Time for Action

Time for Action

Sexual abuse, the Churches
and a new dawn for survivors

The Report to Churches Together in Britain and Ireland
of the Group established to examine issues of Sexual Abuse

CHURCHES TOGETHER
IN BRITAIN AND IRELAND

Churches Together in Britain and Ireland
Inter-Church House
35–41 Lower Marsh
London SE1 7SA
Tel. +44 (0) 20 7523 2121; Fax +44 (0) 20 7928 0010
info@ctbi.org.uk or (team)@ctbi.org.uk
www.ctbi.org.uk

ISBN 0 85169 281 8

Published 2002 by Churches Together in Britain and Ireland

Produced by Church House Publishing

Further copies available from CTBI Publications,
31 Great Smith Street, London SW1P 3BN
Tel: +44 (0) 20 7898 1300; Fax: +44 (0) 20 7898 1305;
orders@ctbi.org.uk www.chbookshop.co.uk

Cover designed by Church House Publishing
Typeset by Liaison Design and Print
Printed by Creative Print and Design Group, Ebbw Vale, Wales

Contents

Figures

Members of the Group on Sexual Abuse set up by Churches Together in Britain and Ireland

Revd David Gamble (Moderator). Representing the Methodist Church in Britain. Pastoral Care and Personal Relationships Secretary. Convenor of the groups that produced the Reports to the Methodist Conference on *Sexual Harassment and Abuse* (1997) and *The Church and Sexual Offenders* (2000). Chair of Barnardo's Council (1997–2002). Currently vice chair of the National Family and Parenting Institute.

Beth Allen. Represented the Society of Friends and was General Secretary of the Quaker Life Department. Resigned after the second meeting when she took on new responsibilities.

Ms Ruth Badger. Represented the Church of England. When appointed was Assistant Secretary of the Board for Social Responsibility with responsibility for relationships with the Child Support Officers in the dioceses of the Church of England. Left after two meetings to work for the Church Commissioners.

Major David Botting. Represented the Salvation Army when their Child Protection Officer in the United Kingdom. A qualified social worker who spent 15 years in residential childcare and worked in H M Prison Dartmoor with section 43 offenders. Attended the first three meetings and then moved to an appointment in Singapore.

Revd Thaddeus Birchard. Appointed as a special consultant to the group. An Anglican priest who is a registered psychotherapist, currently in practice as a psycho-sexual therapist. He has done research into causation and prevention and the overlap between sexual behaviour and religious behaviour.

Mr Nicholas Coote. Appointed to the Group whilst Assistant General Secretary to the Catholic Bishops' Conference of England and Wales. Retired from that position after two meetings but received the papers and attended one of the final meetings to approve the report. A member of the Catholic Bishops' Working Party on the 1994 Pastoral and Procedural Guidelines on the causes of the sexual abuse of children involving priests, religious and other church workers and the 1996 Church Report: *Healing the Wounds of Sexual Abuse.* An observer at the Nolan Review of child protection in the Catholic Church in England and Wales.

Revd Kathy Galloway. Representing the Church of Scotland, of which she is a minister, a practical theologian and a liturgist. Recently appointed leader of the Iona Community. She is a member of Vashti (Scottish Christian Women Against Abuse), an ecumenical agency established with the support of NEWS (Network of Ecumenical Women in Scotland). She previously worked for Vashti setting up a network of Persons of Trust to support women who have experienced abuse in a religious context or with a religious dimension. She has written and spoken extensively on issues surrounding abuse.

Mrs Elizabeth Ingram. Appointed by the Church of England to take the place of Ms Ruth Badger. Bishop's Representative to the Bishop of Peterborough and the Bishop of Ely, advising both dioceses and developing policies, practice guidelines and training for churches in child protection. A member of the Child Protection Liaison Group which advises the House of Bishops and Archbishops' Council on policy and good practice guidelines. A chartered psychologist and Chief Executive of Family Care, a Peterborough Diocesan Charity undertaking independent residential and day risk-assessment with families for social services departments and the Courts where there are serious child protection issues.

Mr Dean Juster. Appointed by the Salvation Army to take the place of David Botting. Has worked for the probation service and as senior social worker for a local authority. Now employed as Child Protection Advisor for the Salvation Army in the UK and Ireland.

Ms Margaret Kennedy. Appointed by CTBI. A nurse and social worker by background and training. The founder and coordinator of Christian Survivors of Sexual Abuse (CSSA) and Minister and Clergy Sexual Abuse Survivors (group) (MACSAS). A professional trainer and consultant in child protection. The author of *The Courage to Tell* and currently researching for a PhD into clergy abuse of adult women in the UK and Ireland.

Very Revd Dr Houston McKelvey. Representing the Church of Ireland. Former Secretary of the General Synod Board of Education (Northern Ireland) with responsibility for the introduction and continuing support of the Church's child protection programme. Dean of Belfast since June 2001.

Revd Barry Osborne. Representing the Congregational Federation, which he has recently served as President. A member of the Federation's Mission and Society Committee. Has worked extensively for many years as an ecumenical rural mission consultant, researcher and lecturer in rural church life.

Ms Kate Prendergast. CSSA support and advice worker. A social worker/counsellor; external examiner and former senior lecturer in Social Work Education; former social services team manager (children).

Ms Sylvia Scarf. Representing the Church in Wales. Now retired but worked in the probation service for many years including a time in residential work in an approved school for children with special needs. Also been involved in Intermediate Treatment (IT), the Youth Bureau, The National Organization for the Treatment of Abusers (NOTA) and the Guide Association. Currently the chair of the Advisory Panel to the Bishops of the Church in Wales on matters of abuse.

Ms Eileen Shearer. Representing the Roman Catholic Bishops' Conference of England and Wales. Appointed Director of the Catholic Office for the Protection of Children and Vulnerable Adults (COPCA) on 14 January 2002. A qualified social worker; worked for the NSPCC for 16 years, most recently as Regional Director South West Region. She was able to attend the last two meetings of the Group.

Revd Jean Mayland (Secretary). Anglican priest. Coordinating Secretary for Church Life at Churches Together in Britain and Ireland.

Ms Trudy Thorose (Administrative Secretary). Senior Secretary, CTBI.

Foreword

This book is not intended for easy reading in the comfort of a fireside chair! It is a book with a purpose and that purpose is to challenge, to call for action and for justice.

Its subject is sexual abuse and the Churches. Its main theme is the Churches' failure as yet adequately to respond to the needs of those who are survivors of such abuse.

Over the past decade there has been increased awareness of sexual abuse as something which happens, even in church circles. In response, most Churches have worked hard to produce effective child protection policies and procedures. Some Churches have also considered how to respond to people who have committed sexual offences when they wish to become part of the church community.

However, far less has been done to date to provide the necessary ongoing support for those who are survivors of sexual abuse. Their stories have been hard to tell and remain so. They are not stories that others want to hear, because they are painful and threaten many of the assumptions on which Christian communities base their common life. They become even harder to hear when we realize that many survivors have not only experienced sexual abuse but often the telling of their stories has been met by denial or rejection. In effect, they have experienced what some have described as 'double abuse', first at the hands of the original perpetrator and second by the refusal or inability of the church to hear their story and respond appropriately.

In 1999, CTBI published the stories of a number of survivors in *The Courage to Tell*. In many ways the current book, *Time for Action*, is a follow up to that publication. It takes the stories of survivors seriously as a starting point for theological reflection and recommendations for positive action on the part of the Churches.

Time for Action affirms much that is already being done to make churches – and wider society – safer places. But it also challenges the Churches both to offer better support to those who have been abused and create an environment where abuse is clearly unacceptable and far less likely to occur.

The members of the Group that has produced *Time for Action* recognize the pain of those who have been abused and who have lived with their stories unacknowledged for far too long. No one can now pretend that these things do not happen or that they are not important. Now is the time for all of us, churches and individuals, to take our stand and to commit ourselves to change. Now is the *Time for Action*.

David Gamble, Moderator of the Group

Acknowledgements

Our warm thanks go to the individuals who gave of their time to attend meetings of the Group on Sexual Abuse in order to make presentations and discuss issues.

We also owe a tremendous debt of gratitude to the members of the Group who were prepared to give of their time to attend frequent meetings and do vast amounts of work in between them.

In particular we express our most grateful thanks to the Revd David Gamble, the Moderator, who chaired with skill and charity meetings, which at times were quite difficult, painful and even stormy.

We thank those member Churches of CTBI, which were ready to nominate members of the Group and also pay their expenses for a long series of meetings.

We thank Lesley Macdonald, currently lecturing at Glasgow University for her work and support as consultant to the Group.

We are grateful to the staff of the various retreat and conference centres that hosted our meetings and ministered to our needs.

We are grateful to the following for permission to use material for which they hold the copyright. Every effort has been made to trace and contact copyright holders. If there are any inadvertent omissions we apologize to those concerned and will ensure that a suitable acknowledgement is made at the next reprint:

Anglican Consultative Council: extract from R. Williams, Address given at the Lambeth Conference, 1998. The Anglican Communion News Service.

Aquarian, an Imprint of HarperCollins: extracts from P. Rutter, MD, *Sex in the Forbidden Zone: When Men in Power Abuse Women's Trust,* 1990.

The Archbishops' Council: extracts from Board of Social Responsibility of the Church of England, *Meeting the Challenge: How Churches Should Respond to Sex Offenders,* 1999.

Bantam Books, USA: extract from P. Carnes, *Don't Call It Love,* 1991.

The Bible Societies: Scripture quoted from the Good News Bible published by the Bible Societies/HarperCollins Publishers Ltd., UK © American Bible Society 1966, 1971, 1976, 1992, 1994. Used with permission. Texts from the Good News Bible, Collins/Fontana, 1976.

Cairns Publications 2000:, 'Light in the dark places', from J. Cotter, *Waymarks; Cairns for a Journey, Unfolded from thoughts of George Appleton, Charles Williams and Julian of Norwich.*

Child Protection Task Force – CORI: extracts from *Ministry with Integrity: A Consultation Document about Standards in Pastoral Ministry,* 2001.

Darton, Longman and Todd: extract from R. Williams, *On Christian Theology,* 2000; extract from R. Williams, *Resurrection,* 1982.

The Diocese of Oxford: extracts from *The Greatness of Trust . . . The Report of the Working Party on Sexual Abuse by Pastors,* 1996.

The Diocese of Southwell: extract from section 5 on 'Perpetrators of child sexual abuse' contained in *Children and Young People First,* December 1999, and now part of the revised version of the Code of Practice for the Diocese of Southwell to protect children and young people and to respond to those who may present a risk to them.

The Free Press, New York: extract from D. Finkelhor, *Child Sexual Abuse,* 1984.

Fortress Press: extract from W. Brueggemann, *Texts That Linger, Words That Explode,* 2000.

HarperCollins: R. Radford-Reuther, *Women Church: Theology and Practice of Feminist Liturgical Communities,* 1985.

Hodder and Stoughton, London: extract from M. Boulding (trans.), *The Confessions of St Augustine,* 1997.

Kirkelig Resurssenter: poem by EH from resource leaflet for *Misshandlede Kvinnor.*

Lexington Books, D. & C. Heath & Co.: extracts from M. Fortune, 'Forgiveness: the last step', in A. L. Horton and J. A. Williamson (eds), *Abuse and Religion: When Praying Isn't Enough,* 1998.

J. Mead: 'Woman without a name' from *Dreaming of Eden,* edited by K. Galloway.

Mowbray: E. Fairbrother 'Collect for Purity', from H. Ward and J. Wild (eds), *Human Rites,* 1995; extract from P. Jamieson, *Living at the Edge: Sacrament and Solidarity in Leadership,* 1997.

Oxford University Press: verse of hymn by D. Harding from *Baptist Praise and Worship,* 1991 copyright © Stainer & Bell, 1969.

Pandora Press: J. Herman, *Trauma and Recovery: From Domestic Abuse to Political Terror,* 1988.

Paulist Press: extract from Richard Gula SS, *Ethics in Pastoral Ministry,* 1996.

Publisher unknown: prayer by M. Melin, from *Karleken en bro (Love-a-Bridge).*

Sage Thousand Oaks: J. Gonsiorek, section entitled 'Assessment for rehabilitation of exploitative health care professionals and clergy', in J. Gonsiorek (ed.), *Breach of Trust: Sexual Exploitation by Health Care and Professionals and Clergy,* 1995.

Source Books CA: 'The sharing' from E. Gateley and R. Chinnici, *Psalms of a Lay Woman,* 1996.

SPCK: extract from K. Galloway, 'Shame', in K. Galloway, *Talking to the Bones,* 1996.

Stainer & Bell: © June Boyce-Tillman, 'We shall go out with hope of resurrection', 1993.

WCC Geneva: extract from M. Kanyoro, *Your Story is My Story, Your Story is Our Story,* 1999.

Westminster/John Knox Press: extracts from by K. Lebacqz and R. Barton, *Sex in the Parish,* 1991.

Wild Goose Publications: 'Survivors' © J. Hulin and 'Inscription' © Rosie Miles from *Praying for the Dawn: A Resource Book for the Ministry of Healing,* 2000.

W.W. Norton and Company: extracts from M. R. Peterson, *At Personal Risk: Boundary Violations in Professional–Client Relationships,* 1992.

And for allowing us to use their previously unpublished work for which they hold the copyright:

'Walking with God in sorrow and need' © Penny Stuart; 'Let us see and hear the truth' © Jayne Scott.

CHAPTER ONE

Introduction: How *Time for Action* came to be written

The issue of sexual abuse has come to the fore in the last few decades. High-profile cases have highlighted the abuse of children in their own homes and in institutions run by both Church and State. As a result much attention has been given by both the State and the Churches to the protection of children. In 1993 the Home Office produced *Safe from Harm,*[1] which gave important guidelines. Many Churches produced their own codes of practice based on these guidelines.

One group, however, feel that their concerns have not been heard – namely those who experienced the sexual abuse, the victims and survivors who have been left to live for many years with their dreadful pain. Their concerns and challenges have been raised by self-help groups such as Christian Survivors of Sexual Abuse (CSSA), founded and coordinated by Margaret Kennedy, a Roman Catholic lay woman.

In 1999 CTBI published a book entitled *The Courage to Tell,*[2] based on the stories of members of CSSA who had suffered from sexual abuse. In the prologue Sheila Cassidy wrote:

> I have thought for some time that the issue of sexual abuse by Christians is the issue for today's Church, in the way that the problem of AIDS patients was the issue that hit us ten years ago. It is an issue that will not go away and which the Christian Church must take seriously.

One of the storytellers wrote:

> I would like the Church . . . to take sexual abuse seriously, not to hide behind a veneer of silence but speak out where sexual abuse occurs. To recognise sexual abuse is a sin committed by the offender, not the victim.

At the launch of the book in York in October 1999 a number of people who had experienced sexual abuse expressed pain and dissatisfaction about the pastoral care which they received from the Churches and asked that a code of practice be established by them. The Church Representatives' Meeting (CRM) of CTBI gave attention to these issues at its meeting in November 1999. After some discussion the CRM passed the following resolution:

Appreciating the work already done by the Churches in this field, the meeting agreed to invite the Churches to share together information about the measures being taken, so that we can seek to identify, formulate and make known an agreed ecumenical approach to these serious matters. To assist with that process, the Churches are invited to address the following questions:

1. In what ways do they give attention to the issues raised by survivors of sexual abuse and provide suitable opportunities for survivors to tell their stories?
2. How do they make available suitable pastoral care for those who have suffered abuse?
3. What mechanisms do they have for 'handling' complaints of sexual abuse made against those who work professionally for the church?
4. What study, discussion and advice about issues connected with sexual abuse is included in the training programme of ministers?

The replies to these questions showed that although the Churches had given attention to the protection of children, work on sexual abuse of adults was much less developed and much needed to be done to provide more adequate care for those who had been sexually abused either as adults or children. The Methodist Church was one Church which had done a great deal of work in the whole area of violence and abuse, but they still reported: 'It may well be that one area that deserves further concentrated work is our response to survivors. Work could be done on this ecumenically and the Methodist Church would gladly be involved in it.'

It was also clear from the responses that more attention needed to be paid to the selection and training of ministers and clergy so that they could give appropriate pastoral care to those who had been abused. Potential clergy needed to be carefully screened so that they did not become abusers themselves.

In the light of these responses the Church Representatives' Meeting agreed that a group should be set up, to be moderated by the Revd David Gamble of the Methodist Church, to work on the pastoral care of those who had been sexually abused and on the issues of confronting abusers. The Group was also asked to reflect theologically on the issues raised by sexual abuse.

At the meeting of CTBI's Steering Committee in September 2000 this brief was further clarified and the Group was set up to consider a wide range of issues connected with sexual abuse. These included:

- the pastoral care of those who have been abused;
- issues of repentance, forgiveness and reconciliation;
- matters connected with the rehabilitation of paedophiles and others committing sexual abuse;
- factors which lead people – including clergy – to become abusers;
- training and supervision.

A group of twelve people was set up and asked to produce a report with recommendations on these issues to be presented to the CRM at its autumn meeting in 2002. The first meeting of the Group on Sexual Abuse (GSA) took place at the Grail, Pinner, from 3 to 4 December 2000. Since then the group has met eleven times more. We devoted much of our first meetings to reflection on theological issues and this undergirded the whole of the rest of our work.

One of our meetings took place in Scotland, one in Wales and one in the Republic of Ireland. The rest of the meetings took place in or near to London as this proved to be the best location for travel from the four nations. Members of the Group took responsibility for certain aspects of the issues and prepared presentations, which were subject to rigorous debate. Papers and resources were shared and examined. A number of hearings took place at which particular aspects of the issues were considered.

At the meeting held at Scottish Churches' House, Dunblane, we heard evidence from three women from different Christian backgrounds who had all suffered sexual abuse by persons respected within the institutions of the Churches. At the meeting in Abergavenny, Wales, we were privileged to have the presence of the Most Revd Dr Rowan Williams, Archbishop of Wales, who spent time with us discussing the theological section of our report. We also heard a presentation by Sir Ronald Waterhouse who chaired the North Wales Tribunal, which considered the abuse of children in care homes in North Wales during the period 1974 to 1996. We were then able to ask questions and discuss with him the implications of his presentation for the Churches.

We met in the Avila Centre, Dublin, during the week in which Bishop Brendon Comiskey resigned because of publicity and demonstrations concerning child abuse by Roman Catholic priests. His work was taken over by Bishop Eamon Walsh who had been due to address us. In the place of Bishop Walsh, Mr John Morgan, the vice chair of the committee set up to assist the work of the Child Protection Office, came to speak to us. He was accompanied by Father Paul Murphy, the principal of the Conference of Religious, who spoke about abuse within religious communities and the measures being taken to deal with it.

We also met with John Kelly, the founder of 'Survivors of Child Abuse – Ireland' (S.O.C.A. – Ireland) who had himself suffered abuse in an industrial school. He was accompanied by Marie Soe, the secretary of S.O.C.A. and herself a survivor of sexual abuse. In addition, Owen Keenan, the chief executive of Barnardo's, Ireland, described the recent history of these issues in the Republic and gave an analysis of and comments on the situation now unfolding.

At meetings in and near London we had addresses or presentations by and conversations with the following:

Two presentations at successive meetings by Donald Findlater of the Lucy Faithfull Foundation, which worked exclusively with sexual abusers. In addition Donald worked in the related Wolvercote Clinic, a residential centre for the treatment of sex abuse. The Wolvercote Clinic closed in July 2002 and a new location is being sought for this invaluable piece of work. On his second visit Donald was accompanied by Ms Val Sheenan. Both spoke of the 'Wolf Sexual Assault Cycle' (see Fig. 2 on p. 94). On each occasion Donald played (with permission) video tapes of sex offenders who are clergy or youth leaders talking, which raised a number of vitally important issues.

We heard a presentation by Ms Gillian Thomas, the chair of the National Association of People Abused in Childhood (NAPAC), which is setting up a helpline with assistance from the Broadcasting Support Services.

At the December 2001 meeting we had a presentation by the Revd Stephen Parsons, an Anglican priest who is the officer of the Bishop of Gloucester for the healing ministry and the deliverance ministry. He is the author of *Ungodly Fear*,[3] which describes the control exercised over individuals by the leaders of some of the more extreme fundamentalist groups. His book also contains criticism of exorcism and other practices sometimes forced upon survivors of sexual abuse.

A feminist analysis of sexual abuse was given to us by Ms Hilary McCallun, who currently works for the Hackney Council Women's Unit. Before that she worked in the Cabinet Office on the National Strategy on Violence Against Women. She has campaigned on issues of sexual abuse for 15 years. She herself suffered violence in a religious context.

At a meeting at the North Bank Centre, Muswell Hill, we heard from the Revd Tony Parry, an ordained minister in the New Testament Church of God and the leader of a Barnardo's project in Bradford. He spoke to us of his experience of dealing with issues of sexual abuse

with Afro-Caribbean Churches in Yorkshire. At the same meeting we
had a discussion with Metropolitan Police Detective Chief Inspector
Tim Bryan. He is currently seconded to the National Probation
Directorate to work on the new arrangements to set up Multi-Agency
Public Protection Panels. Tim is also a minister in secular employment
of the Church of England and Child Protection Adviser in the Diocese
of Southwark. He was involved in the Wolvercote Centre and took
Communion to some of the people there. It was at the North Bank
Centre we came across the poem 'A People Place', reproduced (with
permission) on this page. The members of the Group feel this describes
the kind of places we hope and pray churches will come to be.

During 2002 there has been intensive discussion and much work
in small groups and drafts have been thoroughly discussed and
amended. The issues discussed are difficult ones and the Group itself
has faced its own difficulties in dealing with them yet at the same time
it has worked hard and creatively and in a spirit of friendship. All the
meetings were set in a framework of worship, prayer and reflection,
which formed a vital basis for our work together.

The Report and the recommendations are now offered to the CRM
and to the Churches as a tool to help them to care more appropriately
for those who have been sexually abused and also to enable the
Churches to become more fully the just, open and caring communities
which we believe God wants them to be.

A People Place

If this is not a place where tears are understood
Where can I go to cry?

If this is not a place where my spirit can take wing
Where do I go to fly?

If this is not a place where my questions can be asked
Where do I go to seek?

If this is not a place where my feelings can be heard
Where do I go to speak?

If this is not a place where you will accept me as I am
Where can I go to be?

If this is not a place where I can try to learn and grow
Where do I just be me?

Attributed to William J. Crockett

CHAPTER TWO

In the beginning was the story…

Christ is like a single body, which has many parts; it is still one body, even though it is made up of different parts . . . if one part of the body suffers, all the other parts suffer with it . . . (1 Corinthians 12.12-26)

It is sixty-three years since the first rape when I was three. It happened again when I was five, and again when I was a mature woman of thirty-six.

The first rape was perpetrated by a stranger, a young man from the local sawmill who had sawdust in his crinkly red hair and in the creases of his leather shoes. I did not understand what was happening to me. I felt awful fear and pain. I thought I had been split up the middle. As in most cases of child rape, I believed him – that he had the power to search me out anywhere if I dared to tell anyone. I hid for hours in a backgreen coal bunker until a neighbour discovered me. My dress, clean on that day, my pants and socks were stiff with blood – and something else, a thick substance, which had a smell. She was drunk but kindly, washed me and my clothes, and then took me by the hand to my mother, pleading that I had been playing hide-and-seek, and not to punish me. I think she guessed the truth but, as far as I know, did not share it with my mother.

The second incident involved the breaking of my trust because the man was a courtesy uncle of a friend. He lured me with chocolate, a luxury in those war years. Again there was fear and pain – and shame, followed by the agonizing inability to tell. This man's skill and patience in 'preparing' me were such that I did not suspect his intentions until it was too late. By the time the red light blazed he had me tied to his bed in an attic room. An extra legacy from this was a feeling of guilt, of self-disgust.

At thirty-six I was taken totally by surprise and knocked unconscious. This time I informed the police, and was deeply humiliated for my efforts. 'Had I been wearing something titillating at the time?' was the first question put to me. My anger and longing for revenge were boundless. By then, I was more enlightened by press coverage of this type of crime, but the guilt and self-loathing persisted.

It was only when an elderly friend confided that she did not know why I was not totally unhinged and bitter and twisted by my experiences that I realized for the first time that there had indeed been some kind of healing. We discussed it, and her gentle questioning led me to recall my 'good witnesses', people who had found out about these shameful happenings.

An infant Sunday school teacher, perceptive and observant, had evidently cared enough to read the signals I was sending out. I look back now and recognize the subtle ways in which she affirmed me with a huge injection of love. All this she did while battling with cancer, although I did not know this at the time. She gave me her Bible, a slim, leather-covered book with gold-edged pages, her initials embossed on the front. It smelled of lavender, her smell, and became a treasured possession. I was bereft when she died so soon after our special times together when she kept me behind after Sunday school, and read and sang and talked to me. I am forever in her debt.

Of course, my very good witness was she who had initially touched on the subject of these traumas. But for her, I would never have lowered the net and trawled up those memories from the depths, would never have been able to experience the revelations of healing which continued to come through friends and associates. Those people, through their encouragement and love, enabled and strengthened me.

When I started to write creatively, it became clear that here was a way to benefit from a type of self-help. Teachers and other writers inspired my trust. Gradually, painfully, I began to record events. Tears choked me as I met the final test of reading aloud my own words. After years of reliving those times through committing them to paper, the cutting edge of my writings lost some of its lethal sharpness.

Until a couple of years ago, there had been one sticking point which constantly plunged me into a morass of despair and doubt as to whether I would ever 'recover' in the way which I regarded as the pinnacle of achievement. It was this. Having watched documentaries and read articles about 'forgiving and forgetting', I had concluded that I could forget, but forgive? Never! Convincing psychotherapists seemed to indicate that both were necessary for full, lasting healing. I simply did not have it in me to pardon what those rapists had done to me. And then one blessed, Christ-centred friend, a woman the same age as myself, summed it all up for me in one sentence. She said, 'It's not for you to forgive, Sylvia; leave that to a higher power.' Relieved of this onerous responsibility, I was plucked from that barbed hook. I bless that wise woman.

The pain eased. The acid of resentment became alkaline. It was not a smooth journey. There were many trips and falls along the way, but through patient insistence that I could be in no way to blame, had never invited the rapes, and was now a 'clean' worthwhile woman who would eventually feel able to shed a legacy of suspicion and bitterness, I recovered and became a survivor rather than a victim – which I had thus far felt myself to be.

Thirty years ago I would never have believed this possible. Not everyone in a like situation has had the benefit of the only real treatment for this kind of abuse – love. My heart goes out to them. I am so fortunate to have known the nurturing of those few people. They have, through their gift of love, at a time when I felt so unlovable, healed the memory.

This is the story of a survivor of sexual abuse.

Sexual abuse is not new. It has occurred all over the world, in every age and culture and religion. It should be of concern to all people of goodwill. But the particular context of this report is the Christian Church in the UK and the Republic of Ireland. Among the millions affected by sexual abuse, whether as people who have survived, people who have perpetrated abuse, or people close to either, are many who are part of the Christian community.

People who have survived sexual abuse are at the heart of our remit and the spirituality and theology of those who have survived is the lens through which we look at the Christian community. The perspective from which we write is an intentional one. As the Group was originally set up in response to the challenge and pain of those who have been abused we considered it most appropriate to write from their perspective rather than from that of the Church institutionally or of the academy or of those who have perpetrated the abuse.

An important part of our remit is to describe the conditions that would create a safe environment in our communities of faith in which all, children, women and men, can live without fear, in the mutual respect and dignity that accords with our creation in the image of God. It is also to envision the Church as a sanctuary in which people who have survived sexual abuse will be able to tell their story, be heard effectively and respectfully, be accepted and welcomed and have their suffering and struggles, physical, mental, emotional and spiritual, recognized and valued.

Unfortunately, such conditions do not at present exist to a degree which can be considered reliable. This fact has been the impetus for our report.

Under a thin veneer of normality, the sheer scale and extent of sexual abuse creates a climate of vulnerability and fear, which shapes the daily experience and relationships of us all. Each time a woman is afraid to go out at night; or a man is wary about showing affection to his daughter; or a woman squirms in silent embarrassment at her colleague's offensive comments; or an abused child is too frightened to tell what is happening, witness is borne to the deep distortions at the very heart of our corporate life.

If sexual abuse is not new, neither is the desolation of those who have experienced their abuse in a church context, or sought help from a church, which has failed them. Too often, abuse has not been clearly and unequivocally named as sinful betrayal. We cannot begin to imagine the burden of pain and suffering which has shamed unnumbered victims into silence. But in our time, there are survivors of sexual exploitation and abuse who want to claim their right to justice. They are coming out of the shadows of isolation and despair, and are speaking with righteous anger while looking for a new dawn. Their voices challenge the Church, as the body of Christ in the world, to respond with compassion and courage. Now is the time for action.

CHAPTER THREE

Preparing the way: agreeing definitions and parameters

The Group on Sexual Abuse considered carefully the nature and extent of our remit and we tried to achieve clarity in our definitions and consistency in our terminology.

Clarifying the remit

We took the view that our remit was to consider sexual abuse within the Church, particularly within the member Churches of CTBI, as well as other Churches and church organizations, similar to, but unaffiliated to CTBI.

Recognizing that different member Churches have different organizational and leadership structures, we tried to apply what we have done in a generic way across all the Churches whatever their ecclesial polity.

We have not limited our focus to the clergy, church officials or employees. We have included any circumstances and relationships within a church where there are differentials of power and where that power differential is a function of a pastoral or ecclesial structure.

We recognized, with concern, that there are many varieties and types of debilitating abuse and discrimination in the Church: e.g. physical, emotional, intellectual, financial, social, class and gender. We, however, limited our consideration to sexual abuse only. In doing this we are aware that sexual abuse is in the context of, and related to, other issues of power and authority in the Church and wider society.

Our main focus is on those who have experienced abuse, with reference to those who have perpetrated it where appropriate.

The term 'those who have experienced abuse' refers to:
- children who have been sexually abused
- adults sexually abused as children
- adults sexually abused as adults.

We also draw attention to the amount of sexual and physical abuse that has been perpetrated upon disabled women and men in our society. This is an important matter and we raise it as something of grave concern.

We took the view that we had a primary duty to hear, recognize and bear witness to the needs of people who have been sexually abused and to call the Churches to give a high priority to their pastoral response to abused people.

We were particularly concerned with the points where sexual abuse intersects with the life of the Churches in the following ways:

- where the abused person is a member of a church;
- where the person who has abused is a member of a church;
- where the person who has abused holds a position of leadership or prominence in a church;
- where the Scriptures and doctrine have been used to explain, justify, excuse or in any way legitimize sexual abuse;
- where sexual abuse has taken place within church establishments; organizations, institutions, property, or in any context under the auspices of the Church.

We do not focus our attention on the current sexual abuse of children because work is already being done by others within the Churches and by specialist child protection agencies. We do not want to repeat what others are already doing and doing so well. Where appropriate, we make reference to and endorse that work and encourage the Churches to study and implement the recommendations of these specialist organizations and working parties where they have not yet done so.

We seek to emphasize, that on current evidence, most sexual abuse is perpetrated by adult males on females. We are, however, aware of female to male sexual abuse and same gender sexual abuse so we agreed that our report would include these patterns of behaviour. We noted, with concern, that the homophobia widely found in some of our churches is another form of abuse and is equally unacceptable. In particular we regretted the tendency to make assumptions that gay men are more likely to abuse boys. We recognized that heterosexual men sexually abuse boys.

In our view, the response of some of our Churches to the call to accountability in the matter of sexual abuse has been exemplary. The creation of policies and procedures to minimize the incidence of sexual abuse has been diligent and immediate. In many cases the Church's response has been in advance of other charitable, voluntary and statutory agencies. We call on all organizations to develop good practice and to avoid complacency.

Other Churches have been less responsive and we noted this with sadness and contrition. Our goal has been neither to apportion blame nor to criticize but to call the Churches to responsibility and accountability. In so doing, we call the Church to its inherent mission and its responsibility as the Church, to be the Church, with faithfulness and integrity.

Defining the terms

We have reviewed the work of others in defining sexual abuse and have included some of this in our understanding of the nature of sexual abuse.

The forms which sexual abuse take can include incest and child sexual abuse, rape and other forms of sexual violence, sexual harassment, unrealistic and degrading representations of women, pornography, trafficking in and prostitution of women, girls, boys and young men, female genital mutilation, sexual violence in war, sexual contact or sexualized behaviour – whether physical, verbal or non-verbal: innuendo, comments, insults, jokes, propositions, threats, suggestive sounds, leering or obscene gestures. The essential feature of abuse is that it is not welcome, mutual or consensual. It is unwanted by the recipient. Sexual abuse or harassment is often a deliberate, premeditated process, rather than a single act. The fact that a child may appear to welcome inappropriate sexual contact because of the 'grooming' process or preparation for abuse is further abuse of the child's right to healthy social and emotional development and appropriate sexual contact.

Sexual abuse and harassment in a church context also includes the sexual exploitation of church members, colleagues, students, young people, children or people seeking pastoral support, where the very nature of the relationship precludes meaningful and informed consent.

Those who experience sexual abuse may be of any age, male or female but are predominantly girls, boys and women. Adults are often abused at vulnerable times in their lives – times of crisis, bereavement, illness or incapacity – however it should not be concluded that abuse *only* happens at such times or to particular kinds of people. It can happen to anyone.

We recognize that abusive sexual behaviour always involves differentials of power.

Language

We agreed that the language used in our report would be clear, inclusive, respectful and non-oppressive.

Throughout this paper we use the term 'abuse' to mean sexual abuse except where the context makes this clear.

We note that the vocabulary applicable to sexual abuse is not in common usage in the public context let alone in some church communities. We are aware that such language can be shocking or disgusting to those who have not been abused. We keep in mind that people who have been abused have been propelled unwillingly into this area of knowledge and this is a cause of further abuse. We ourselves do not lose our innocence in gaining such knowledge; we lose our ignorance and become more able to support and be part of the healing process.

Sexual abuse is a physical, emotional, mental, psychological and/or spiritual criminal assault or injury that has a range of repercussions. Those offended against will display some or all of the effects to varying degrees, depending on the impact of the event at the time or later.

We considered using other terms like 'victim', 'survivor' and 'perpetrator', but in the end, decided to use 'people who' as our term of choice where we could do so without straining language too much. While we recognized other terms are current, and often self-applied by individuals and groups of individuals who have been abused, in our view, the term 'victim' and the term 'survivor' created 'less-than states' and brought with them suggestions of ongoing disempowerment. People who experience abuse are offended against, are targets of abuse, are subjected to abuse and are survivors of abuse. One person who had been abused described himself as existing with the experience because he could not identify with the positive connotations of having 'survived'. The term 'victim' has assumed negative connotations reflecting a prejudicial view of people who have been targeted by sex offenders. Survivors describe themselves as victims, survivors or (recovered) thrivers.

We therefore agreed generally to use the term 'people who abuse' and 'people who experience abuse' to designate the correspondents when writing about abuse in this report. This was agreed because of the importance of keeping in mind that we are, in all cases, dealing with people, and thus, with all their rights, dignities and inalienable sacredness. We felt it important to remember that, in both cases, people should not be defined, in their entirety, by either term.

We were also cautious about using the word 'paedophile', which is problematic and gives the impression that sexually abusing children is a sexual orientation, thereby giving some validity to the offence. A person who sexually abuses a child is a criminal, a sex offender who targets children, who are vulnerable and powerless in relation to adults.

We also recognized that there will be individuals and groups who will have enabled or allowed the abuse to have taken place. Where this has been done by ignorance or indifference we have used the term 'enable'. Where this is more active and conscious we have used the term 'contribute'. These are all people, groups and organizations, who share responsibility with people who abuse, for the impact of these behaviours on those who have been abused both at the time and later in their lives. In this regard we had in mind, within churches, as both 'enabling' and/or 'contributing', the following conditions and circumstances among others:

- culpable ignorance
- silence
- gagging
- covering up
- failures to respond
- an absence of supervision and accountability
- the absence of teaching and training for those in positions of leadership.

In Chapter 8 of the Report, where we speak of abuse within the Church we have referred to sexual exploitation by the clergy.

By this we mean:

- sexual harassment
- hugs, kissing, fondling, groping
- masturbation/digital penetration
- sexual intercourse (vaginal and anal)
- oral sex
- rape
- involving a person in the making of pornography or 'encouraging' a person to view pornography.

We recognize that there will be individuals and groups who will also be harmed by this behaviour, either directly or indirectly. We use the term 'others harmed' or an appropriate equivalent. Others harmed by abuse include the person who abuses but also: families, friends, colleagues, congregations and communities. In this regard we had in mind, within the Churches, the following consequences and outcomes among others:

- harm done to the name of Jesus Christ;
- harm done to the good name of the Church;
- the wholesale impairment of the Church's credibility and effectiveness in proclaiming the gospel in its ministry and mission. Too much protection of the Church's 'good name' harms the good name.

We recognized that the Churches' peculiar structure, their ethos of forgiving sin and not thinking badly of anyone, coupled with the taboo on openness about sexuality and sexual activity, make them easy arenas for those who abuse in which to 'groom' their targets.

We also recognize that abuse within the Church has unusually grave consequences in that it has the possibility of alienating the people who have been abused from the content and context of their faith community and thus from sources of ultimate purpose, meaning and solace.

Ethical Commitments

We recognize the power of language to distort, minimize and oppress and therefore have sought to take particular care to avoid the use of language that devalues or minimizes others, and to seek to avoid, in this report especially, language that is sexist, or that fails to describe people with disabilities with due respect.

Sources of information

These are acknowledged wherever possible.

Confidentiality

We have only used information in the public domain or where explicit permission has been given.

Diverse understandings

Many of the issues and experiences dealt with in *Time for Action* are highly sensitive and painful. They are also open to different interpretations and understandings. As a Group, we reflected a wide diversity of experience and expertise and members sometimes differed considerably in their understanding of the issues. This reflected the fact that everyone is bound to bring to their discussion of these matters their own perspectives and sometimes quite painful experience. The text of this Report is an agreed text, but not all members of the Group would be equally comfortable with every part of it. This diversity of experience and understanding will also be shared by those who read the Report.

A word of warning

We decided to include considerable detail in describing some of the behaviours involved in sexual abuse and in some of the consequences experienced by those involved. The detail is included to help develop awareness, especially for those engaged in pastoral care. However, this is not a textbook and it is important for any pastoral carer to be aware of their limitations. When a person has been sexually abused it is always good practice to involve other professionals and agencies with the appropriate skills and expertise. The potential further damage caused by someone operating 'out of their depth' must be avoided at all costs.

CHAPTER FOUR

Setting the scene

The Group on Sexual Abuse was set up by CTBI mainly to consider the needs of those who have been offended against, and they are the major focus of this report. However, it is important to look at the wider context in which the work of the Group is set – as this throws important light on what is happening in our society today. This chapter seeks to do this.

Sexual exploitation and the abuse of children are no new phenomena but have appeared in various forms throughout history. Just over a century ago, in the 1880s, Josephine Butler and Florence Booth (appalled at the sale of Eliza Armstrong, a 13-year-old daughter of a chimney sweep, for £5 for use in a brothel), campaigned to expose what they called 'white slave traffic'. As a result of their campaign the Criminal Law Amendment Act raised the age of consent from 13 to 16 years old. The work of these and other social reformers in the late nineteenth century also led eventually to the setting up of societies for the prevention of cruelty to children.

In the early twentieth century there was little public attention given to these issues. After the Second World War the debate was about links between 'maternal deprivation' and 'juvenile delinquency', with a concern about the implications of inadequate parenting for society as a whole.

The last 30 or 40 years have seen a dramatic increase in public concern about violence and abuse both against children and within the family. The year 1962 saw the publication of *Battered Baby Syndrome* by Henry Kempe, which focused attention on the physical abuse of children. There were a number of high-profile cases of physical abuse of children in the UK during the 1970s and 1980s (e.g. Maria Colwell and Jasmine Beckford), and during the 1990s in Ireland (e.g. Kelly Fitzgerald and the McColgan family), in some of which the children actually died. Horror was expressed at what some children experienced in their own homes in a supposedly civilized society. A major concern was the ineffectiveness of social services departments and other agencies in offering protection to children and the agencies' failure to draw information together. Still far too many children are not safe in their own home, as the recent high-profile enquiry into the death of Victoria Climbié has shown.

Meanwhile, in the 1980s the focus of public attention moved on to the sexual abuse of children, although again much of the media and political debate (e.g. in the 'Cleveland Crisis' in 1987) was over the role played by public authorities and whether the medical, social work and other professionals interfered too much or at the wrong time (too late in cases of physical abuse and too early in alleged cases of sexual abuse) in private family life. The role of professional and statutory agencies continues to be difficult and controversial. Some have suggested that too much public money is now spent on protection and intervention at too late a stage, rather than on more general early preventative work and improvements in child welfare or development of children's rights.

In the late 1980s and early 1990s some media attention was devoted to stories of abuse with 'ritual' or 'satanic' overtones, and of so-called 'paedophile' rings and networks.

Although concern has continued over children at risk in their own homes (highlighted in the NSPCC's 'Full Stop Campaign' in 2000–2001), during the 1990s some of the attention moved to allegations of abuse that had taken place within the setting of children's homes and other institutions. A number of enquiries were held into allegations of abuse in such places, going back over a long period.

In May 1999 the Irish Government apologized to victims of institutional abuse and subsequently established a Commission to Inquire into Child Abuse, chaired by Judge Mary Laffoy. A compensation body was set up for victims of historical institutional abuse. Some high-profile cases have led to the imprisonment of priests and other people in positions of authority. Churches and other groups throughout society misunderstood the nature of abusive behaviour. Too often the assumption that repentance and absolution would lead to reformed behaviour led merely to moving those who abused to new areas of work and those who had been abused were overlooked. The Irish Government concluded an agreement with the Catholic Church on the contributions to be made (both in the form of cash and assets) by the relevant religious bodies to the compensation 'fund'. Some victims' groups and elements of the media have criticized the agreement on the grounds that the Church's contribution is too small.

There is a wider international dimension to this and in the United States and Canada some historic abuse cases have led to huge compensation settlements which have threatened the existence of some churches and religious (and other) organizations.

Over the past few years a new area of concern has developed over what is sometimes called 'indirect abuse', with the use of the Internet for the distribution and exchange of child pornography. The making of such images involves the direct and terrible abuse of children. Internet 'chat rooms' have also been used to entrap children. The Internet crosses international borders, so children in the UK and Ireland can be affected by the activities of people in countries with different laws regarding sexual offending, the age of consent, etc.

All this is set in a historical setting in which, at the beginning of the twenty-first century in Britain and Ireland, there is a very different social climate regarding matters of sex and sexuality than just 50 years previously. The parameters have changed in what is seen to be acceptable behaviour. Films, magazines, newspapers and advertising all use sexual imagery very openly, often closely linked with explicit portrayals of violence. Although there may be some public acceptance of the concept of the 'new man', an equal partner in the home and fully involved in matters of parenting, housework, etc., the media continue to use strong images of a more sexually dominant and violent way of seeing masculinity.

It is also worth noting that during the period of writing *Time for Action* there were regular high profile news stories of people in authority (in government, business, etc.) abusing their power for their own ends.

An environment where such stories become commonplace to the extent that they cease to amaze, and where sex and violence is regularly portrayed on TV screens in most homes is part of the wider context in which the sexual abuse that is the concern of this Report takes place.

People's stories

In recent years, many adult survivors have started to speak about their experiences of abuse during their childhood, often disclosing things kept secret for 30 or 40 years. At the same time, there has been increased stress on listening to the voices of children. Organizations like NAYPIC (the National Association of Young People in Care) and its Irish equivalent IAYPIC have told of young people's experiences; ChildLine (set up in 1986) has provided an opportunity for children and young people to tell of their own experiences; and the Children Act 1989 and parallel legislation gave legal recognition to children's right to be heard on matters that concern them. Devolution in the UK has been followed by discussions relating to the possible appointment of children's commissioners (such as the one newly appointed in Wales) as another way of ensuring that children's voices are heard. The Irish Government has published proposed legislation for the establishment of an office of Ombudsman for Children. This has been before the Oireachtas and has recently passed into law.

We have also heard the stories of adults experiencing domestic violence. The UK Government, in its 1998 consultation paper *Supporting Families,*[1] named this as one of four major family problems to be addressed. *The Way Forward,*[2] a report before the Methodist Conference in 2002, looked at the Church's involvement in and response to this issue.

Attention has been given to appropriate ways of enabling those who have been abused to give evidence in court, as a public hearing in the presence of the person accused of abusing can be a very threatening experience. It is believed that only a very small proportion of abuse cases end up in court and the difficulty of gathering and presenting evidence is one reason for this. However, there is much contention about this and it is sometimes argued that the relatively small number of allegations that lead to convictions suggests that many false or unsubstantiated allegations are made. Some have also argued that some of those who make allegations of abuse that took place many years in the past, do so as a result of what is often called 'False Memory Syndrome'. As a Group we are not persuaded by this argument. Having considered it very carefully, we have come to the view that there are many reasons why those who have been abused remain silent. These are hard stories to tell and even harder to prove. There are fears that a person's experience will be denied and not believed. And the person who has committed abuse has done so from a position of relative power over the one who has been abused. Given all the factors that make telling the story difficult, it is likely that many experiences remain secret. This is not, of course, to suggest that allegations of abuse are never false or unfounded but we believe all allegations must be taken very seriously.

The Republic of Ireland's Commission to Inquire into Child Abuse has established a two-track approach. There is a public, contested forum for the hearing of stories/allegations and a Confidential Committee, which hears and records people's stories, which are not contested. For some former residents this has seemed to provide an appropriate resolution, in so far as their story has been told and heard and is on the record but remains confidential.

Public legislation

There have been various government initiatives and responses in the Republic of Ireland, the UK and its three national parliaments and assemblies. Mention has already been made of the Children Act 1989 in England and Wales, the Children (Scotland) Act 1995 and the Children (Northern Ireland) Order 1995. Jersey passed similar

legislation in its Protection of Children Act 1994. In 1993 the Home
Office produced *Safe from Harm,*[3] setting out guidelines for good
practice in organizations working with children. Similar
recommendations were contained in the Scottish Office's *Protecting
Children* (1995). The 1990s saw recommendations followed by
legislation for the registration of sex offenders. In 1999, the
Department of Health, Home Office and Department for Education
and Employment issued a revised version of *Working Together to
Safeguard Children: A Guide to Inter-agency Working to Safeguard and
Promote the Welfare of Children.*[4] This advocated greater cooperation
and partnership between different statutory and voluntary agencies,
and with families and the wider community. Area Child Protection
Committees are examples of this increased cooperation. They have
also issued a national *Framework for the Assessment of Children in
Need and their Families* which complements *Working Together* and
prescribes an inter-agency process.

In 2002 the Criminal Records Bureau came into operation,
enabling organizations working with children to check the criminal
records of potential staff and volunteers.

There have been similar developments in the Republic of Ireland,
with a Child Care Act passed in 1991. *Children First: National
Guidelines for the Protection and Welfare of Children* were published in
1999 and in the same year the Protection of Persons Reporting Child
Abuse Act and the Child Trafficking and Pornography Act came into
force. The Sex Offenders Act 2001 created a register of sex offenders,
made it an offence for an offender not to declare the conviction, and
allowed orders to be made for supervision of those discharged from prison.

In addition to legislation directly relating to sexual offending and
child protection, there has been other legislation with indirect
influence. In particular, data protection and human rights legislation
affect the treatment of those against whom allegations are made and
limit ways in which information that is not in the public domain is
shared. The Freedom of Information Act in the Republic of Ireland has
raised concerns about the need to ensure reports to the authorities are
marked 'privileged'. The full effects of this legislation will not become
clear until case law develops.

It is also true that the Human Rights Act, in so far as children also
have human rights, can be a powerful tool to protect them.

Fear of litigation and its effect

It is sometimes suggested that we live in a very litigious age, where
people with complaints are perhaps too quick to seek legal redress and

financial compensation. Having said that, it seems strange to point the finger of blame at a person who seeks compensation when a crime has been committed against them. However, it may well be that one reason for the decline in numbers of people willing to volunteer to work with children is the fear of litigation. Some fear that innocent behaviour that would have been unquestioned in a previous generation might now be misinterpreted and used as the basis for a complaint followed by legal action. Yet a well-implemented and supported child protection policy offers safeguards not only to children but also to those who work with them. Insurance companies sometimes will not insure churches that do not have child protection policies. At the same time, some survivors are afraid to take appropriate action in case it fails and they get sued. Others keep quiet because they are concerned about the possible consequences for the Church if they blow the whistle.

What churches have already done

Good practice

The Consultative Group on Ministry among Children (CGMC), a CTBI Network, has been working on issues related to the development of good practice in child protection within the life of the Church for over a decade and has enabled those responsible for child protection in the different denominations within Britain and Ireland to liaise.

In England and Wales, the passing of the 1989 Children Act and the guidelines which went with it (and parallel legislation and guidelines in other countries) alerted churches to some of the external demands regarding good practice in work with children and in the appointment, training and supervision of those who work with children in voluntary groups. The 1993 Home Office document, *Safe from Harm*,[5] contained 13 good practice guidelines. Most denominations have produced material and procedures to encourage local churches to implement these guidelines and many have published their own versions of them (e.g. the Church of Ireland's *Safeguarding Trust*[6] or the Salvation Army's *Safe and Sound*[7]).

There is an understanding of the importance of developing good practice in church life and work with children and young people. Doing this helps protect both the young and those who work with them. One aspect of good practice involves procedures to be adopted to try to ensure that unsuitable people are not allowed to work with children. Following the Police Act 1997 systems have been set up to enable much wider access to police checks, or Disclosures, as they are now called. Throughout the UK there was concern that charging for these Disclosures would make the process very expensive for churches, so the Government's decision to drop the charge for volunteers (though not employees) was well received. There is also some concern that people may put too much trust into such a system of checks, when many abusers of children currently have no record.

The Criminal Records Bureau came into operation in the early part of 2002 for those requiring Disclosures in England and Wales. There is the same opportunity for those living in Scotland through Disclosure Scotland, set up by the Scottish Criminal Records Office. Churches will apply through registered or 'umbrella' bodies. In some cases the body will operate on behalf of a denomination or diocese. The Churches' Agency for Safeguarding will function on behalf of a group of denominations initially brought together under the auspices of CGMC. In Northern Ireland denominations and the headquarters of youth organizations can register with the Department of Health and Social Services to enable 'PECS checks' (PECS denotes Pre-Employment Consultancy Service) to be completed for adults working with children and young people. This is completed by the department in consultation with the police, who also network with the system operated in the remainder of the United Kingdom. There is no charge for this service. A similar procedure is developing within the Republic of Ireland.

The Catholic Bishops' Conference in England and Wales accepted the recommendations of Lord Nolan's Review Committee Report, *A Programme for Action*,[8] in November 2001, and has established the Catholic Office for the Protection of Children and Vulnerable Adults (COPCA), which will act as the 'umbrella body' for CRB checks for the Catholic Church in England and Wales.

Training and awareness building

In 1992 the National Children's Bureau published its *Taking Care*[9] pack (latest edition 1997), a response to children, adults and abuse for churches and other faith communities. The pack was produced by staff of the Bureau working with representatives of the Churches and the Christian childcare agencies. It sought to increase awareness about child abuse, offer guidance to churches in how to protect children and support families in stress, and provide information and advice on responding to adults with childhood experience of abuse or adults involved in abusive situations. The pack has been well used and its use has often provided opportunities for adults to share their stories of current and past experiences. In Northern Ireland, a similar pack has been produced.

Over the past ten years child protection and related issues have become increasingly part of the training both of those working with children and young people and those preparing for diaconal and presbyteral ministry. Churches have come a long way. But there is still a very long way to go, both in increasing awareness within the Church as a whole and in ensuring that all those with particular responsibilities in these matters are fully prepared and supported in their role. What is more, training is not a one-off event but needs to be an ongoing and repeated process.

Those who have offended

Some Churches have also addressed the issue of how to incorporate people with convictions or police cautions for sexual offences into their congregations (see Chapter 10). Over the past three years the Church of England and the British Methodist Church have published reports. In the Roman Catholic Church in England and Wales, Lord Nolan's Independent Review Report *A Programme for Action*[10] deals with this along with its wider child protection recommendations. The published reports contain some reflection on theological issues, suggest procedures for the incorporation of offenders in church communities, consider some of the factors that lead to offending behaviour and make recommendations regarding awareness building, training and supervision. The Society of Friends has some involvement in developing what are known as *Circles of Support*, helping to reintegrate people who have offended and offer them a supportive network of people to help them rebuild their lives.

Given that abuse sometimes occurs within the church context, attention has also been given by the Church in Wales and the Church of England to matters relating to clergy discipline legislation and the Methodist Church has brought in new complaints and discipline procedures. The Roman Catholic Church is in the process of implementing the *Programme for Action*[11] in this respect, and clergy against whom allegations are made now take 'administrative leave' while statutory agencies investigate, and where risks are thought to persist thereafter are removed from active ministry.

Those who have been abused

The preceding pages have shown how much has been done by the Churches to improve their practice, to develop training and increase awareness, and to consider how those who have offended may be involved in church communities without creating unnecessary risk for previous or potential victims. However, much more needs to be done.

In particular, there has so far been little targeted and specific response by churches (or, indeed, society at large) to the ongoing pastoral needs of victims/survivors, or to the abuse of adults by clergy and others.

In 1994, the Roman Catholic Church in England and Wales published a document on the effects of abuse within the Church on child victims of sexual abuse, entitled *Healing the Wounds*.[12] The Methodist Conference 1997 *Report on Sexual Harassment and Abuse*[13] majored on the experience of adults, though it also dealt with certain matters to do with abuse of children. This acknowledged that the issues surrounding abuse are not just to do with children. In addition to new complaints and disciplinary procedures for the Church, there were recommendations relating to the provision of better systems of recruitment, training, support and supervision for those in positions of responsibility and pastoral oversight in churches.

Time for Action seeks to redress the balance and address the needs of those who have suffered both at the hands of those who have abused and because of the churches that have been unable or unwilling to listen to them.

What people who have survived sexual abuse have done

It is recognized that it has been the courage of people who have survived child sexual abuse in speaking out about their experiences that has let us know fully the depth and breadth of child sexual abuse. In speaking out they have informed their friends, family, colleagues and therapists what it is to be sexually abused in childhood. Only then could specialists develop a picture and conceptualize the dynamics of sex offending and effects on the victim. The movement to protect children, therefore, has been spearheaded by those who have themselves experienced abuse and therefore have not wanted other children to go through what they have experienced.

As well as this courage to 'speak out' survivors have largely been responsible for setting up support networks and voluntary organizations throughout the UK and Ireland. For example, most of the Rape Crisis centres which now cater for those who have survived child sexual abuse were established by rape victims since the statutory services failed to address adequately their needs. The Broadcasting Support Services have published an excellent *Survivors' Directory* with large numbers of these groups and organizations in it. There are still very few therapeutic resources for adult survivors of child sexual abuse within the statutory services. What there is tends to pathologize the victim as 'ill' and services are located within psychiatry and psychological therapeutic centres or hospitals. While these are helpful, not all survivors want to be considered as 'mentally ill', for a great many are not!

Christian Survivors of Sexual Abuse (CSSA) and Minister and Clergy Sexual Abuse Survivors (MACSAS) are interdenominational groups and were founded by a person who has survived child sexual abuse and clergy abuse. CSSA self-help support groups exist in London, Oxford and Gloucester and these are run by people who have survived sexual abuse. They have organized religious services, retreats and literature to support and inform both the Churches and other people who have themselves experienced sexual abuse. CSSA has produced a booklet called *Safe Church – Safe Children*[14] and a beautiful prayer card which helps people to remember those who have been abused whether as children or adults. CSSA's wallhanging, 'A visible sign of our presence', is depicted in the book, *The Courage to Tell*,[15] published by CTBI – and is available for showing in churches.

Certainly many people who have survived sexual abuse have informed their churches as to their needs and *some* churches have developed spiritual and pastoral support in response.

S.O.C.A. (Survivors of Child Abuse) has been set up both in Ireland and the UK to assist people who were abused by clergy in Irish industrial schools.

One in Four was founded by a person who survived clergy abuse, to support others, who were abused by a range of different sex offenders both religious and lay.

The National Association of People Abused in Childhood (NAPAC) was also founded by those who have survived abuse and aims to offer a nationwide (UK) service to help people to find the most helpful service or resource.

The Bristol Crisis Service for Women has been set up to offer support to women in emotional distress, particularly women who self-injure. They have a national helpline, produce information packs and leaflets and offer training days on working with people who self-injure.

Vashti – a charity set up by Scottish Christian Women Against Abuse to offer support to women who have suffered or are suffering abuse in a Christian context, has now been 'live' for a year. Following the official launch a number of enquiries were received and although the service has not been inundated with requests for help there has been a steady trickle of enquiries throughout the year. With the Persons of Trust network covering most of mainland Scotland and Orkney, Vashti continues to develop and is accessible to all areas.

CHAPTER FIVE

It's hard to hear but harder to tell

There are some things people would rather not hear. It may be that the information being received generates emotional pain or disgust. It may be that hearing another person's story stirs up deeply buried memories in our own lives. Or it may be that, as we become aware of the consequences of what we are hearing, the enormity of it overwhelms us.

There is no doubt that many find it hard to listen to or read stories of sexual abuse. But that should make us aware that the stories are not normally easy to tell. There is deep-rooted fear of being misunderstood, of feeling that at least some of the blame for what was wrong may fall upon the one who has been abused, thus adding to the pain already suffered. It is therefore not surprising that there are many, quite apart from those who commit abuse, who would rather everything was left buried and undisturbed.

Silence is a key tool that enables those who abuse to do so. It will never stop unless we find the courage to listen to what others need courage to tell. Rising to this challenge will not be easy and is certainly disturbing, but until the Church faces up to this issue it will be failing in an important part of its life and responsibility.

There is another aspect that challenges our attitude towards that which is hard to hear. The voices of those who have been the victims of abuse often contain tones of anger at the injustice of Churches and Christians who would apparently rather stop their ears or who offer inappropriate responses both to those who suffer from abuse and those who commit abuse. Listening to anger towards others is one thing, but it is harder to cope with when it is anger towards ourselves.

Sometimes when voices are raised in anger it is not easy to hear the words above the passion. Those who clamour for our attention need to be aware of this difficulty, for we need to hear their pain, to understand its causes and learn how to help in the healing process. On our part, perhaps we need to acknowledge that often the voices are raised when too many people cannot hear because they have their heads buried in the sand.

Who are those who survive sexual abuse?

It seems probable that experience of sexual abuse in one form or another is far more common than is generally acknowledged. This would imply that those who survive sexual abuse are among us even though, for the main part, they remain unrecognized. People with whom we work, worship and socialize may include those who survive sexual abuse. Often, when a survivor finds the courage to make known something of their story, people respond by saying, *'I would never have guessed'.*

This gives rise for both encouragement and concern: concern that the problem is so prevalent but encouragement because many who have been sexually abused achieve a high degree of normality of life.

We have deliberately chosen to speak of those who survive sexual abuse (see Chapter 3), for there is a life beyond the moment or moments of abuse and it would be unhelpful to remain identified as a victim and to be somehow locked into that identity. The effects of sexual abuse are deeply traumatizing so, for those who have found the resources to move on beyond the actual experience or experiences of abuse, to rise above it (even though the scars may remain), some pride may be taken in the achievement.

While those intent on sexually abusing others seem to have no difficulty in identifying potential targets, society is often slow to recognize those in danger or shocked to discover that almost anyone could become a victim of sexual abuse. There is a deviousness among some of those who sexually abuse that enables them to identify and home in on those who are vulnerable.

But most sexual abuse is not committed by extreme deviants; it often takes place within the home, from 'caring' people within the family and within other contexts in which there is an expectation of trust and care. In other words both those who are abused and those who abuse may be more ordinary than some would expect. Even genuine care and affection can develop a deviant or unhealthy nature, which it why it is important that appropriate boundaries of behaviour are set and maintained.

In the recent past much more has become known about the abuse of young children; however, sexual abuse is experienced by adults too. While there is a tendency to feel anger and sorrow for those very young who suffer there is significantly less compassion for those whom we presume should somehow have known better than to let themselves get caught up in an abusive situation or relationship. Such a view is naïve. Whenever abuse happens it is wrong and deserves condemnation. All those who survive sexual abuse deserve compassion and appropriate levels of support.

There is a tendency for many of those who have survived sexual abuse to keep silence and thereby the degree to which sexual abuse takes place remains covered. However, those whose story has become public testify that subsequently others then find the courage to share something of their stories.

A middle-aged person who had survived sexual abuse in her childhood told her story on a television programme and found that her story had been picked up in a local newspaper. She was surprised when visiting her regular garage for petrol that the attendant commented on how surprised she had been to read the account. She then confided that she too had been sexually abused but had never dared to tell anyone.

A middle-aged minister who suffered sexual abuse as a young man within a para-church mission organization struggled with the issue of reporting the person who had abused him to the police. He was afraid of the possible consequences to his own ministry. When he became aware of a senior police officer whom he felt he might be able to trust, he sought advice confidentially from a friend who was a more junior police officer. His friend was reassuring and, as the conversation drew to a close, added that he too was a survivor of sexual abuse.

The nature of abuse varies. Those who have never themselves been victims of abuse might consider some acts less serious than others, as do some people who have been abused. But the measure of seriousness should be the emotional impact it causes. For example, 'flashing' may seem trivial to some, but suffering this experience has seriously damaged some people's lives.

Many of those who survive sexual abuse find themselves haunted by dreams and bad memories and feel themselves locked into a private world of pain and distress. Some are too embarrassed to tell anyone about their experience and so may never experience the therapeutic benefits that usually follow supportive counselling and/or acts of justice.

Sexually abused men

The surveys that have been conducted tend to demonstrate that there are more female survivors of sexual abuse than male survivors. There is, however, reason to believe that the incidence of sexual abuse against boys and men is greater than is reflected by the testimony of survivors. One explanation for this would be that male survivors of sexual abuse feel more inhibited in telling their stories. The stories that have come to light may well be just the tip of the iceberg.

For most men, acknowledging vulnerability or weakness of any kind does not fit well with Western male culture, in which men are supposed to be strong and assertive. It is easy to imagine how difficult it would be for them to tell their story of suffering sexual abuse. But men as well as boys fall victim to the devious and manipulative behaviour of those intent on abuse. Some fall prey to threats and physical violence, while others, who have strong empathetic qualities, might have these exploited.

Boys may well grow up being told that sex with men is called homosexuality and if a man abuses them they might believe that they must themselves be homosexual. Negative attitudes towards homosexuality, homophobia, have sometimes led abused boys to be afraid of being thought gay and criticized within society or the church. This can leave a sexually abused boy feeling lost, guilty and confused. While later he may discover that the act of abuse may not have been specifically homosexual, and *certainly did not affect his own sexual orientation*, the shame and guilt built up can remain for years.

Where sexual abuse takes place within a church or Christian organizational context, fear of potential damage to the reputation of the church or organization is powerful. In consequence there may seem to be an obligation to remain silent, and therefore an opportunity either for the abuse to continue or for others within the church or organization to fall prey. The numbers of those abused within a church context may be larger than already recognized because the survivors remain silent among us.

Not just an urban problem

While sexual abuse might appear to be more common in urban areas, it would be wrong to assume that abuse does not take place in rural areas. The lack of anonymity within rural communities may have an inhibiting effect on those who would sexually abuse others but it does not stop it from happening. A teenage girl walking home from an evening job in the kitchen of the village pub in an apparently safe community was followed and raped by two boys who were well known locally. Perversely, because the boys' families were long established in the village, and the girl came from an 'incomer' family, the community offered overt support for the boys to mitigate their punishment, while offering only slight sympathy for the girl. Even during the course of working on this report a relative of one group member was walking her dog down a lane in her village when she was stopped by a man in a car who exposed his erect penis to her.

The 'niceness' of rural communities may lead to denial that anything like that can happen here or, if it does, it must be by an outsider. Such naïvety is dangerous. People in rural churches often feel that because they 'know everyone' involved the churches are a safe place. Such a view is premised on the false assumption that those who sexually abuse are somehow sufficiently different from the rest that they can be spotted.

Because of their smallness, rural churches are often very welcoming to new people attending and gladly accept offers of help. Where human resources are limited it is all too easy to grasp a new offer of help without proper evaluation of risk or investigation. Such an open door provides an opportunity for a predator or a temptation to the weak. We received some evidence that appropriate guidelines for ensuring that churches are safe (such as *Safe from Harm* policies) are less likely to be in place in rural churches, making them potentially dangerous environments.

The intrinsic intimacy of a small rural church or a small rural community also raises problems for providing appropriate responses both to anyone who has been sexually abused or for the reintegration of someone convicted of sexual abuse. The latter may be an insurmountable problem. Living in a village is something like living in a goldfish bowl and the emotional and psychological pressures upon someone who has survived abuse may also become unbearable in such a social context.

Abuse of those with disabilities

In September 2001 the *Guardian* reported that a man accused of sexually abusing a woman with a learning impairment was acquitted. This happened not because the alleged victim could not say what happened, but because the defence barrister said she had such a low IQ that she would not make a 'credible witness'. Yet Liz (not her real name) gave a very clear account including descriptions of oral sex. Her mother said that she could not have known what this was unless she had experienced it. Here is what Liz said herself:

> He had sex on me. He touched my boobs and bottom – don't like it. I told him 'no' but he just kept on doing it. I never told anyone what happened because he said 'don't tell your mummy and daddy or the police'. He was just naughty. He had sex on me in the laundry room and no one saw me. He's plain guilty. I want him back in a prison cell. I didn't get the chance to see the judge. I wanted to tell him what happened to me. He was so silly that judge. I wrote him a letter and said 'please sir, can you help me' but he didn't.

Unfortunately, most witnesses with impairments never get heard in the judicial system as a result of the belief that because of their impairments, they have concomitant psychological or emotional disturbance or other cognitive impairments that would invalidate their testimony. This myth pervades the professional system at all levels. This erroneous but endemic prejudicial discrimination allows large numbers of children and adults with impairments to be sexually abused and assaulted.

While in Britain and Ireland there are no reliable statistics on the extent of the abuse of children with impairments some attempt has been made to look at the issues in Canada and USA. There the research shows that children with impairments are three times more likely to be abused than children with no impairments. In the UK Professor Hilary Browne of the University of Kent at Canterbury estimates that 50 per cent of people with a learning disability have probably been sexually abused at some point in their lives. Sullivan *et al.*[1] state that in the USA 54 per cent of deaf boys and 50 per cent of deaf girls have been sexually abused in childhood. There is no reason not to assume that the same figures would be true for the UK.

There are many reasons why children with impairments are made more vulnerable to abuse. The word 'made' is used because for the main part the 'cause' of vulnerability is not their impairment but the structures and attitudes of the environment around them.

Lack of value as citizens

The protection of children and adults with impairments has not been given adequate consideration and this has resulted in there being almost no specialized safety programmes appropriate to their needs (e.g. using Braille, sign language or in accessible English for people with learning impairment).

Might lack of value in society have been a factor in the exclusion of Liz from the judicial process (see story above) because of the additional requirements that would be needed for her full inclusion, which would add to the cost of investigations and the court case? Many adults with impairments have remarked 'it's as if it doesn't matter so much when I'm sexually abused as it does for non-disabled people'.

This was recently revealed in the Westminster Parliament when in response to a question asked by David Hinchliffe MP[2] the Government admitted it had funded no research into the abuse of children with impairments in the last five years. When asked by *Disability Now* (a specialist journal) whether they intended to undertake such research, the UK Government responded with a statement that they did not intend to do such research in the foreseeable future.

Emotional deprivation

Many children with impairments feel that they are not the children their parents wanted. They feel negatively about themselves and have a poor self-image, believing themselves to be defective human beings. This message is given in many ways by society, particularly now as genetic research increasingly suggests that, in future, they will not exist. People with impairments see storylines in television 'soaps' around abortion of impaired babies and articles in newspapers about parents claiming compensation because an impairment was not picked up on scan or amniocentesis, etc. Emotional deprivation makes people with impairments vulnerable to sexual predators who tell them they love them without any conditions.

Care dependency

Some disabled people need hands-on care by numerous people in the course of their day and week. Many disabled children are cared for in residential settings: hospitals, residential schools and respite care homes. We know that living away from home increases risk of sexual abuse because of the numbers of those providing care. Children may need washing, dressing, incontinence pads to be changed, catheters emptied, rectal valium administered, help to get into a wheelchair, creams, lotions, injections given, feeding and physiotherapy. Growing up with such intimate interaction with others may lead children with impairments to fail to appreciate the importance of 'boundaries' and that they alone should have control over who touches them and what is done to them. Where there is good practice staff will demonstrate that they do not have power or control over a child's body and exercise care with privacy, dignity and respect. Poor practice may send a message that what happens to an impaired person is completely outside of their control. Thus they become doubly vulnerable.

Communication difference

Some disabled people do not use voice to communicate. This increases risk. While there are various other communication methods, some people with learning impairment do not have the cognitive skills to employ any sophisticated system and therefore rely on a very restricted vocabulary. Some professionals and parents are reluctant for disabled children to have vocabulary for body parts or about sex or sexuality, thus many children with impairments use 'censored' systems and may not be able to disclose effectively.

The result is that reporting abuse, giving a police statement or going to court becomes more complicated for those using non-verbal communication methods, though for many it would be possible if only the system allowed them to use sign language or other alternative ways of communicating. Most legal personnel, and many Social Services child protection teams have little understanding of these systems and how to use them to best advantage. Training is rarely given.

Parental bias

In the past the model used to work with children with impairments assumed that parents were overwhelmed by difficult and burdensome children. Much effort was put in to support parents and an ethos that facilitated feeling sorry for parents prevailed. This resulted in the voices of disabled children not being heard. The parents' wishes and views took precedence over their children's wishes and views.

In the last few years the rights of children with impairments have increasingly been recognized in law (though there is still a long way to go) leading to a movement from a parent-biased service provision to an equality-driven service, where the needs of both parents and children with impairments are equally addressed. Disabled children are at last seen as at high risk of abuse, possibly from their parents or carers. It is now recognized that children with impairments deserve a 'rights' perspective rather than a 'charity' perspective in their care.

Overview

There are considerable difficulties in relation to the abuse of children with impairments. We know that they are more likely not less likely to be abused and this includes sexual abuse. Adults with impairments are also at risk – a point that has been recognized in the production of a new journal, the *Journal of Adult Protection*, which covers risks from all kinds of abuse.

The Church and disability

Attitudes within churches towards those who are disabled may also contribute unhelpfully to this vulnerability. Jesus Christ was known for curing the sick and people with impairments of his time. The Gospels record both healing from sickness (e.g. leprosy) and healing from physical impairment (e.g. blindness, lameness, deafness, etc.).

The Early Church was also characterized by such miracles and there are claims that they occur today. Regrettably, some enthusiastic Christian Churches and groups practise a methodology in praying for sick and infirm people that is weak in pastoral sensitivity and care. They may also be lacking in theological reflection. Consequently, rather than finding this helpful some have found it further disabling.

Disability is often projected as an aberration of the normal and those who are in any way impaired need to be 'made whole'. Obviously physical fitness is not the only desirable quality for the human condition. Intellectual ability, spirituality and quality of character are equally important and valid factors. To highlight one particular form of impairment more than, or even to the exclusion of, others is deeply offensive.

It is often believed by non-disabled people, that people with impairments would (and should) jump at the opportunity of cure. Many, in fact the majority, do not; accepting their condition, they have learned to live within the restrictions and have developed a positive self-image as proud disabled people. To suggest to people with impairments they should seek cure is anathema to them and in fact outrages them. Unsubstantiated claims by some that they can cure have left people with impairments betrayed or angry and offended. It causes anger that yet again a non-impaired person projects on to an impaired person his or her values and assumptions.

In some churches there still abounds the belief that parents have been 'gifted' by God with an impaired child because they are special people. This concept again offends people with impairments. It suggests that they are such a burden only special people can look after them. An alternative belief in some more extreme fundamentalist groups is that impairment is a result of a parent's sin or evil entering the impaired person. It does not take much for this belief to transmute to 'you are evil'. Extreme care must be exercised when discussing the meaning of impairment and how this fits with the theology of healing. A great deal of additional harm has been caused by beliefs that belong to a bygone age. Our particular concern here is to suggest that poor theology and practice within the Churches relating to disability may be a factor for some in rendering them psychologically vulnerable to abuse.

Churches responding to disabled adults

The following suggestions may help churches to include impaired abused people within their remit when considering pastoral care of sexually abused adults. A good starting place would be to ensure that the church has appropriate policies for responding to the needs of disabled people. Recognizing that children and adults with impairments are more likely to be sexually abused, churches and their organizations must take extra care in respect of any human interaction and assistance that they may need in church.

If it is known that a disabled person has also suffered from sexual abuse, particular sensitivity and wisdom must be shown. There is growing understanding that vulnerable people who have suffered sexual abuse are likely to suffer subsequent abuse. This includes adults who have been sexually abused as children (both non-disabled people and disabled people).

Training is imperative for all persons who have responsibility for the pastoral care of children who are abused and adults who were abused as children.

Breaking the silence barrier

Often people are confused that some people wait many years before they tell their story of abuse. They wonder why this is and become anxious that it might involve a so-called 'false memory'. However it should be noted that the term 'false memory syndrome' has not been recognized as a psychiatric condition nor validated as a scientific process.

In order to understand why it takes years for many victims of child sexual abuse to tell their story it is crucial that the mechanism and dynamics of abuse are understood, particularly to understand how sex offenders 'silence' victims.

Often those who do not understand these 'silencing' techniques have asked those who survive sexual abuse, 'Why has it taken you so long to tell anyone?' Worse still it can be wrongly assumed that the person who has at last managed to break the silence is now being especially vindictive. Another common assumption is that the person who has broken the silence is only doing so in order to get compensation. 'After all,' they are told, 'if it really was true you would have told someone at the time.' Such reactions are based on a failure to understand the psychology of abuse and consequently additionally traumatize many adult survivors.

Secrecy formation

Commonly those who abuse children instil a fear that is so awful that a survivor knows almost instinctively that he or she cannot possibly dare tell another person about what has happened or is happening. Consequently there are deep-rooted feelings of loneliness, isolation and fear.

Such feelings often last well into adulthood. It is not unusual for adult survivors of abuse to continue believing totally in the power of the sex offender, even after the person who abused them has died. Many sexual abusers are skilled manipulators and the use of 'secrecy' and 'silencing' techniques has been well documented by specialists who treat such offenders. Techniques include telling children things that will frighten them, such as: 'Your mother will have a heart attack if you tell'; 'I will kill you/your mother/pet dog'; 'You will be taken into care'; 'Your mother/you will go to prison'. All these messages are given to terrorize the victim into complete silence and to encourage compliance. Clergy sex offenders often use spiritual threats or confusing messages, such as: 'You'll go to hell if you tell'; 'God does not mind what is happening'; 'You will hurt God if you tell'; and 'No one will believe you because I'm a priest'.

Few children are able to withstand such pressure and many retreat into a closed off cocoon, wrapped in a shield of depression, anxiety, and fear. Such emotional and psychological impact of child sexual abuse may last years, even well into adult life.

The physical acts of sexual abuse may also further instil other feelings that block the telling of the story. Shame, guilt, disgust, self-blame and a real belief that if you 'allowed' it to happen you must be at fault, further prevent any breaking of the 'secret'. Girls told by their offender that they are beautiful and seductive can infer that there is something about them that caused their own abuse. This can cause them to retreat further into the silence.

Victims of sexual abuse by women can be especially fearful that no one will believe them and often find it personally shameful to be abused by someone they had perceived as a nurturing figure. Those sexually abused in group sexual acts are usually so traumatized that talking about it may demand very special courage.

Sometimes false guilt and shame contribute to the silence. Sexual acts can generate feelings of pleasure – even within a criminal or abusive situation. The sexual response is outside of one's control and quite natural. However a person being sexually abused may conclude that the arousal and pleasure experienced indicate they must have enjoyed it and therefore wanted it. This adds to guilt, shame and to self-blame. It may take many years and possibly therapy before those who survive sexual abuse understand that sexual arousal or pleasure is not consent.

Aware of the natural sexual response, those who sexually abuse use this to their own advantage in perpetuating abuse. In such a situation any response from an abused child or vulnerable adult is more likely to indicate a need for emotional nurture and not simply a desire for sex.

A person who has experienced abuse may also experience guilt from a belief that they unwittingly caused the abuse of another, or were complicit in the abuse. On some level those who are abused feel that by controlling when it happens they can prevent it happening on other occasions. Some have said, 'I'd go to him on Monday so that I'd be free for the week'. Some 'allow' abuse in order to protect their siblings, following the usually mistaken logic: 'If I give myself then he won't go on to my little sister.' Anyone with knowledge of the ways of those who abuse children and vulnerable adults know too that any feelings of guilt borne by the victims are completely irrational. However, the guilt is real and painful. It becomes another part of the silence trap.

Whether sexual abuse took place upon a child or adult, someone physically, mentally or psychologically impaired or someone who is non-impaired, the story is bound to be unpleasant, and always harder to tell than to hear.

CHAPTER SIX

Listening well to what's hard to tell: responding to those who have experienced sexual abuse

Reminder: This chapter goes into considerable detail to develop understanding on the part of those involved in pastoral care. However, Time for Action is not a textbook and it is important for any pastoral carer to be aware of their limitations. When a person has been sexually abused it is always good practice to involve other professionals and agencies with appropriate skills and expertise. The potential further damage caused by someone operating 'out of their depth' must be avoided at all costs.

Much healing can come from belonging to a safe, nurturing and caring Christian community. This is contingent, however, on the Christian community knowing something about what it is like to be an adult survivor of sexual abuse. Telling one's story calls for enormous courage and a high level of trust. Since it is the nature of abuse to destroy or at least damage trust, it is imperative that when a survivor is ready to tell his or her story the listener must respond with great sensitivity and care.

Adults who have been sexually abused as children fall into two broad groups. Some have developed ways of coping and dealing with the harmful legacy. They may not feel the need to explore their past, nor to identify themselves as people who have survived child sexual abuse. They may wish to leave well alone and to put this part of their life behind them. Some may identify completely as people who have survived abuse, and feel that they have 'moved on' and that coming to terms with the experience of abuse has shaped and coloured the person they have become. One should never assume just because a person has been sexually abused in childhood that counselling or therapy is or should be mandatory. This assumption can be patronizing and negates the personal resilience, strength and courage many survivors have found. Such people recognize that child sexual abuse has harmed them but that abuse is just one part of their lives and not the sum total of who they are.

Other adults who were sexually abused as children may be in need of counselling or therapy. Still others may have entered counselling or therapy already and found a measure of peace. Some need periodic ongoing support of this kind. Those who continue to suffer flashbacks or bad dreams may need particularly sensitive support that can only come from those who have some understanding of the nature of trauma. They may always need support and encouragement in life, in addition to counselling or therapy.

Within each of the broad groups there will be variations. There is a continuum from being a person who still feels a victim to being a person who regards herself or himself as a fully recovered survivor, and wherever those who have been abused see themselves to be they need to be fully accepted. It is imprudent and possibly dangerous for any well-meaning pastor or Christian friend to try to determine progress.

Every person responds differently to child sexual abuse. There is no 'blueprint' of responses. However, there are common 'themes' that are evident in many survivors' lives to a greater or lesser extent. Knowing these difficulties will help in offering pastoral care.

Responding well is the beginning of healing

Speaking about sexual abuse is tremendously difficult for both the survivor and listener. We all have inbuilt defence mechanisms that help shut out pain when it reaches an unbearable level, or prejudices that could impede the ability to listen and respond well. We must first address these tendencies so that we can 'make room' to receive what a hurt and damaged person may need us to receive.

Sex and sexuality have never been easy topics to discuss within church circles. Consequently they become taboo, a private matter with certain moral stances supported by Christianity. In the past we shied away from openly addressing these aspects of human life, but now we are aware that such secrecy has contributed to harm, shame, guilt and erroneous beliefs.

It is important that Christians become more open about the whole beauty and giftedness of healthy relationships, love, sex, sexuality and our bodies in general. 'Body-talk' or 'sex-talk' is a neglected aspect of spirituality and theology for most Christians. The more openly we can address this subject, the better we will be able to address the abuses and misuses of sex that have been so damaging to many Christian women and men.

This report has already made clear that sexual abuse happens to adults of all ages as well as to children. All sexual abuse has negative consequences, but there may be some value in our drawing attention to the consequences of sexual abuse suffered in childhood. While these comments focus on abuse in childhood, many would be equally relevant in situations where sexual abuse has happened to an adult.

The nature of the harm

Children are not equipped to deal with premature sex physically, emotionally or psychologically. Premature sex is therefore harmful. The harm is from two different sources:

a) the physical nature of the sexual acts and immediate psychological consequences, and

b) the psychological and emotional distortions generated by offenders in their attempt to prevent disclosure.

Physical harm and immediate psychological consequences

Some forms of sexual abuse – particularly penetrative sex – might be painful and might injure a child. The child might also develop infections. Their immaturity makes it confusing for them to understand the experience of sexual arousal that might be experienced during an act they may know to be intrinsically wrong. Consequently while arousal can bring pleasure it may also generate feelings of fear, shame and guilt. An adult is usually bigger and stronger than a child or young person. The target, therefore, can be physically trapped quite easily. This disparity of body size and status brings fear. In some situations, even touch can be immobilizing, where it is outside the receiver's control and ignores the receiver's wishes or feelings, and brings feelings of powerlessness. In almost all cases, a child or young person has no ability to do anything about a bigger, stronger person with more power or status who is engaging them in sexual activities that they do not want.

Psychological and emotional distortion

To the fear and confusion caused by the act of sexual abuse is often added further complications as the abuser seeks to manipulate the victim in order to gain compliance and/or to seek to ensure subsequent silence about what has taken place. Those who sexually abuse others commonly have a ready repertoire for engagement, entrapment, abuse and silencing. For example, one silencing mechanism is to convince the child that what has happened was his or her fault. This creates 'self-blame' which is advantageous to the perpetrator.

The combination of the direct psychological and emotional effects arising from the act and distortions implanted by the words of the abuser may have lasting results well into adult life. This not only includes continued fear of telling, but other aspects of psychological and behavioural dysfunctionality.

Issues of trust

Many who have sexually abused children did so when they occupied positions of trust, or were a loved or well-liked person. After being sexually abused a child might not find it easy to trust anyone ever again or become very confused about trust. Some adults who have been sexually abused as children naïvely seek strong relationships and trust too much, which can lead to further sexual exploitation and abuse. This usually happens because the adult has not developed a proper understanding of social boundaries while growing up. Other adults sexually abused in childhood trust too little and can be defensive, distant and unapproachable. This can lead to loneliness and isolation.

Those offering pastoral care and support may find that they will not be trusted or at least not fully trusted. This is the adult survivor's healthy safety mechanism to protect himself or herself. Those who wish to offer care should not expect a person who has experienced abuse to trust them. They will have to prove their trustworthiness.

On the other hand, it is important not to let the survivor develop too great a dependency on those who offer support, for this will limit their personal and social development. Dependency is a feature of trusting too much. Helping a survivor to develop a healthy balance of trust, which enables good social interaction, might be a long process.

Shame, guilt and self-blame

Adults sexually abused in childhood often experience long-term shame, guilt and self-blame. While they may hear words such as, 'it was not your fault; you were only twelve years old' the feelings of guilt and/or shame sown at that time might have so taken root that the adult is unable to take in this message. Children who are older when sexually abused are more likely to blame themselves, even if there was nothing that they could have done at the time. This is particularly likely if the abuse was experienced repeatedly throughout childhood.

Only with time and perhaps counselling or reading about abuse (particularly on how offenders 'groom' and manipulate their victims) might an adult lose a sense of shame, guilt or self-blame. For many these are residual feelings that never completely go away. It is always useful to emphasize to an adult that it was not their fault but this should be supported by reason and informed advice on why the supporter believes this. Knowledge about how abusers of children operate is enormously helpful.

Fears, phobias, flashbacks and panic attacks

Many adults who were sexually abused as children have a level of fear about certain people and life events as a consequence of that abuse. Many live in a super-alert or hyper-vigilant state, ready to flee at any sign of danger or threat. There can be fear of locked rooms, or unlocked rooms; fear of men or women (depending on who abused them or let them down); fear of getting too close or fear of being alone with another person; fear of certain noises; fear of doors closing; fear of dogs barking; fear of certain smells, such as aftershave, drink on the breath, or perfume; fear of certain places such as cars, seaside or cupboards; or fear of being touched.

Such fears can act as 'triggers' for flashbacks. Flashbacks are brief but very real images or memories relating to the experience of abuse. For example, a door bangs and the survivor immediately descends into fear and a vivid memory of her abusing father coming for her. The memory is intense and immediate, and the feelings engendered are very real. Flashbacks can cause regression, the adult might begin to cry or shake as he or she did as a child. It might produce dissociation in which the adult loses touch with the present moment and appears to 'disappear' into a different place.

Such responses might be alarming to the onlooker. Anyone engaging with an abused person who has such a response is advised to keep calm and try to be reassuring. The voice should remain steady, even and firm. It may help to invite the person to tell you what is being felt or remembered (take care only to listen; do not make suggestions). When the flashback has passed try to encourage the person to resume a routine and activity that is neutral and unemotional such as washing the dishes or making a cup of tea.

Sex, sexuality and intimacy difficulties

It is very common for those who have been sexually abused to have difficulties with sex, sexuality and intimacy. Some remain single preferring no intimacy or possibility of sex; some marry or have partners but find sex and intimacy threatening, causing flashbacks and dissociation. Yet others may use their sexuality as a means of numbing pain or as a mechanism for gaining control and power in relationships.

For some women, the loss of control experienced in an act of sexual abuse (perhaps particularly where that happened in childhood and in cases of repeated abuse) may make it difficult for them to commit to a long-term sexual relationship. They seek instead relationships in which they feel that they remain 'in control'. For example, this might be a series of short-term encounters or even prostitution. What manifests itself as promiscuity might actually be a defensive mechanism.

Sexual abuse in formative years can distort a person's understanding of the relationship between sex and general human interaction. Where one has grown up believing that the only way to relate to another person is by being sexual, or realizing that this seems to please people, one may continue to believe, as an adult, that this is what is expected.

All sexual or intimacy difficulties require a skilled and trained therapist. These therapists should abide by ethical guidelines, be under supervision and the person seeking help should be aware of to whom to go if their counsellor or therapist tries to engage them sexually. Pastors, ministers or friendly members of the congregation should never undertake counselling on matters relating to sex and/or intimacy.

Anyone who is in a relationship with someone who has been sexually abused can offer help simply by reassuring him or her that such difficulties are not surprising and that the survivor should not blame himself or herself. Encouragement to seek help from knowledgeable people in the field of sexual abuse should be given.

Pastoral care or healing ministry of people with sexual or intimacy difficulties should never involve engaging that person in any way that is sexual in order to 'heal' them. Such exploitation has been known and is a real problem for survivors who have experienced it both from clergy and other professionals.

Anger and rage

Anger is a not inappropriate reaction within someone who understands that he or she has been the victim of sexual abuse. It may not begin to manifest itself until some time after the event. However anger needs to be expressed in a healthy way, and not all who have been abused are able to do that. Some may come from a childhood home that was not only abusive but also characterized by violence and anger.

Where anger is associated in the mind with the context in which sexual abuse took place, then the person who has been abused may not be able to cope with other people's anger later in life and may suffer an emotional or behavioural reaction to it.

Where a person who has been abused shows periodic uncontrollable anger or a strange reaction to other people's anger then counselling and therapy will almost certainly be helpful, though some develop mechanisms without help for managing such emotions.

Self-harm

Some adults who have been sexually abused as children are so angry they self-harm. Self-harm is any behaviour such as cutting, burning, overdosing, hitting or damaging body parts with implements. Some observers consider eating disorders also a form of self-harm. Usually self-harm is not about suicide but is a way of feeling better when overwhelmed by very strong emotions. These emotions might include anger, rage, shame, guilt or self-hatred. Feeling physical pain becomes preferable to feeling mental pain, anger, shame or guilt for what many survivors believe is 'their fault'.

The pain of self-harm sets off endorphins in the brain, which cause natural 'highs', somewhat like morphine, that can act as a form of anaesthesia. After self-harm, survivors often feel calmer and better. Contracts not to self-injure rarely work and might cause additional problems.

In such situations self-harm is not about attention seeking, nor is it a manipulative act; it is a coping strategy. To fail to understand this could lead to an inappropriate response such as telling a person who has been harming himself or herself that what he or she is doing is sinful or bad. If what they are doing is a means of coping with feelings of guilt or shame, such a negative reaction could only further exacerbate the problem.

Isolation

Feelings of shame or embarrassment following sexual abuse may lead to withdrawal, and consequently isolation and loneliness. Attempts to tell one's story may have been met with a negative response, and this too can result in isolation. There is often a feeling of being different or possibly 'spoiled' by the experience of abuse, or of having suffered an experience that others do not understand – or even want to understand. The fear of being misunderstood or, worse still, stigmatized may also be factors causing withdrawal and isolation.

It is challenging for Christians in our churches to offer appropriate responses to the loneliness and isolation experienced by some of those who have survived child sexual abuse. Obviously positively seeking to include people in activities is important but this will need to be done discreetly. Where a survivor of sexual abuse who has become isolated, suddenly finds himself or herself spotlighted for extra attention, it is likely to exacerbate the problem and not solve it. The isolated person needs to make his or her own journey, though some assistance may be needed. The speed of emergence must be within their own control, and friends should not express concern at any sign of regression.

Sometimes the isolated space is the only safe place someone who has been sexually abused knows. It will take time and patience for trust to develop in the company of others.

A word needs to be said here about physical proximity. Well-meaning people leading church meetings have encouraged people sitting on their own to move closer to another or to others. For someone who has suffered sexual abuse, close proximity may induce terror. Similarly such things as 'sharing the peace' or being encouraged to greet and 'share fellowship' with others in a service might be unhelpful. Isolation is sometimes a tool chosen for reasons of security.

Powerlessness and lack of confidence

Sexual abuse is always about an improper and unreasonable exercise of power by one person over another. Especially where such abuse has taken place over a period of time during the formative years of personality the sense of powerlessness might result in a child never feeling confident enough to be assertive. Such traits that continue into adult life can lead to further exploitation and abuse. This further abuse might not be of a sexual nature; it might be seen in social relationships within work or home, or among 'friends', where others take advantage of apparent weakness.

Confidence and self-esteem may be so low they can cave in under the slightest bullying or verbal or emotional assaults – even teasing. Such survivors are vulnerable to manipulation by others, financially, personally, sexually and spiritually.

Good pastoral care can offer new skills to survivors within the church community where they can begin to take responsibility for aspects of community life with support. This might mean helping at Sunday school, joining or leading a home group, or reading prayers or Scripture in a public service.

Sleep

Night-times can be particularly bad for those who have suffered sexual abuse. Going to bed can resurrect memories and/or flashbacks that cause sleeplessness and fear. Nightmares or night terrors are not uncommon. Panic attacks are also more common when tired or alone. It is at night that some survivors need the most support and yet they must, because of reality, learn to cope whether alone or with a partner. It is never good pastoral care to say 'ring me whenever you need me'. It does not create safety or appropriate boundaries, and can foster dependency. It is important for those who are helpers or supporters to give a limit on being called upon by survivors. Survivors might be very needy but also must develop their own self-care skills.

Survivors can call helplines during the night and the Broadcasting Support Services produce an excellent *Survivors' Directory* so that anyone needing help can get ready access to helplines or support groups.

Loss and grief

There is a great deal of loss following sexual abuse, such as loss of childhood, loss of innocence, perhaps loss of family, home and siblings if taken into care, loss of safety, loss of confidence, loss of self-esteem and loss of trust. Such losses may lead to great sadness and depression. Those who feel such losses may even feel that they caused them, particularly where the loss resulted from their reporting the abuse. If the depression reaches the lows of total hopelessness then there is urgent need for skilled help. Good pastoral carers should always be alert for the signs of such extreme depression.

The Christian gospel is a message of redemption and recovery but it is naïve to presume that all that has been lost can be compensated for by friendships within a church. For example, the church community can be a place to 'belong' but it is not able to replace natural family relationships. Some survivors have experienced more problems when they try to make the church fellowship into the family they never had. The truth is that the grief for family loss is there forever and must be worked with, not covered over with the 'wallpaper' of church life. Good things about church life should be understood as 'additional to' and not as 'substitution for'; getting it wrong could delay the process of grieving.

While recognizing that adults sexually abused as children might find considerable support and benefits through the fellowship and ministry of churches, we have also identified some of the difficulties. To maximize the potential benefits those in leadership must work towards a better understanding of the problems and train that they might the better respond to the needs.

Some reactions are beyond control

Sometimes the behaviour and reactions of someone who has been abused may seem strange, irrational or extreme. Not all reactions are possible to control. Human beings have physiological, emotional, mental and spiritual responses to all experiences. Some experiences are processed with little complication but some present the whole system and personality with severe challenges. Sexual abuse is understood to impact on all levels of functioning in the person abused.

Physiological responses

One response that has caused great distress to abused people is the physiological response. Like many other creatures human beings might experience what is usually called a 'fight, flight or freeze response' whenever a serious threat is perceived. It is an unconscious, involuntary reflex reaction. The body prepares itself by releasing adrenaline for physical activity. For humans the physiological reaction occurs in response to any kind of perceived threat – not just physical threat. So in the case of sexual abuse the body's autonomic nervous system reacts according to the level of fear generated by that experience. This autonomic system governs reflex actions all over the body. The responses are normal, if uncomfortable. For some the response is severe enough to cause a degree of temporary 'freezing' with inability to act or to articulate properly. It is important to keep in mind that the autonomic nervous system does not discriminate; if a threat is perceived to be life-threatening then the response is in accordance.

If the symptoms are not acknowledged and not dealt with appropriately they can persist. In such cases the slightest reminder of the original cause can reproduce intense fear. Autonomic responses can also be triggered by events unrelated to the abuse and ostensibly of no great significance. Such responses obviously appear irrational to others and the sufferer might be accused of overreacting. Such attitudes from others generate further distress.

Because the autonomic nervous system operates throughout the body, discomfort or pain could be felt in any organ or tissue. For example any one or a combination of the following effects may be felt: extreme pain in the abdomen, stomach or solar plexus, severe throat constriction, cramp-like pain in the chest, palpitations in the heart, headaches, fear of fainting or falling, severe sweating or blushing. Even the simplest of these or other symptoms may well generate distress since the sufferer cannot control them. Once the sufferer begins to understand that these are normal reactions beyond their control, that realization in itself can begin to bring relief. A sympathetic response by those around helps recovery, while an unsympathetic response may exacerbate the problem.

Psychological and emotional responses

For the victim, when abuse occurs it causes trauma on all levels of functioning. Denial of the experience can manifest itself in repression of the memory, that is the 'shelving' of the experience until the person is able to attempt to process it in a safe place. This is analogous to the experiences described when someone has suffered significant physical trauma: the wound is numbed, anaesthetized, and the person carries on performing heroic feats before eventually feeling the immense pain. The emotions, too, can be numbed, frozen for varying lengths of time and when this effect lessens the person will respond emotionally according to their perception of what has happened.

Processing traumatic events

Sexual abuse has a traumatizing effect. While this is felt most acutely by the person who is the victim of the abuse, others such as those associated with the person who has been abused, or those associated with the person committing the abuse, and even the person committing the abuse, are affected and have to 'process' their reactions. To help explain the way in which the various reactions are processed, we provide the following diagram.

This diagram is based on a model for understanding the processes involved in dying and bereavement developed by Elizabeth Kubler-Ross, which has been adapted to incorporate the processes involved in the experience of sexual abuse.

Figure 1. Processing abuse.

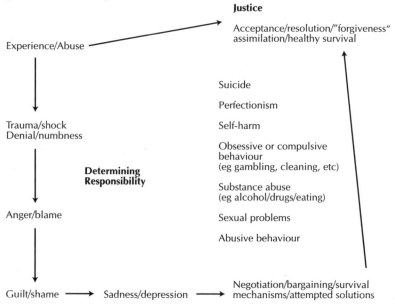

The diagram above illustrates the emotional and behavioural responses to the experience of sexual abuse. It is based on the processing of any human experience of significance to the individual.

We consider below how the processes work in each of four categories: on the person who has been sexually abused, on those associated with the person who has been abused, on the person committing abuse, and on those associated with a person who has committed sexual abuse.

Effects on the person who has been sexually abused

There is the event itself, then the responses of the individual physically, emotionally, mentally and behaviourally. These responses are further affected by the responses and behaviour of others, such as the person who committed the abuse and those close to him or her. If the person who committed the abuse has not accepted and assumed responsibility for his or her actions or if no third party has affirmed that the person who committed the abuse is entirely responsible for what has taken place, then the guilt and the shame associated with the action can be, and often are, unconsciously assumed by the person who has been abused.

The anger and blame that would naturally be felt and expressed by the abused person is often suppressed through fear and lack of knowledge until the experience can be processed in the light of further knowledge or maturity.

Suppression of the emotions demands exertion of energy. On the diagram the line from the traumatizing event to justice could be understood as similar to the lid on a pressure cooker. If responsibility for sexual abuse is not assumed by or allocated to the abuser the inherent injustice gives energy to the inappropriate guilt assumed by or allocated to the abused person. This energy fuels the anger and shame of the abused person who may continually repeat the cycle of these emotions or undergo feelings of depression. Should the depression not result in suicide the person who has been abused then has to negotiate ways of living with often intolerable anger, shame, depression, and disabling and painful physical anxiety. This is where 'survival mechanisms' or 'attempted solutions' come into operation.

Survival mechanisms or attempted solutions include a variety of behaviours. We indicate here some of the possible ways in which an abused person may act as they seek to come to terms with their trauma and pain. Every individual's response is his or her own – conditioned by many things. We do not imply that every sexually abused person will manifest any of the behavioural responses, but we do assert that such responses are far from uncommon.

For there to be an appropriate response to someone who has been sexually abused it is essential for there to be first an understanding of why there may be some problematic behaviours. It would be naïve for it to be assumed that anyone showing any of the behaviours shown in the diagram and commented upon below is only doing so consciously to attract attention to themselves; they are ways of coping with pain. The list is not prioritized in any way and some elements may be more obvious than others:

- suicide
- self-harm
- mood-altering substance use (e.g. alcohol, drugs, etc.)
- mood-altering behaviour (e.g. gambling, video games)
- obsessional behaviour (e.g. cleaning)
- problems with sexual activity (e.g. avoidance of sexual relationships, multiple casual sexual relationships, or prostitution)
- abusive behaviour.

Similarly mood-altering behaviour, the use of mood-altering substances, and obsessional behaviour are attempts to 'bury' the emotional pain.

Problems with sexual activity are dealt with earlier in this chapter of the Report.

The possibility of a sexually abused person engaging in abusive behaviour needs special comment. Abuse here might include various forms of abusive behaviour, physical, emotional, sexual, etc., and might be a symptom of repressed anger. Some of those who have been abused may themselves later show abusive behaviour. It must, however, be noted that the vast majority of those who have been sexually abused never abuse another person. Indeed, on the contrary, there is significant evidence that their experience is more likely to result in their becoming more caring and careful people.

A person can become 'stuck' at any stage in the emotional and behavioural processing of the experience of abuse and can move backwards and forwards between the stages as they negotiate their thoughts, feelings and behaviour in relation to the experience. If a person is stuck in the phase of attempted solutions these can shift the focus and become the main problem diverting attention from the original, unresolved problem. The original problem, however, cannot be resolved until the attempted solution ceases to be the focus.

Effects on those in contact with a person who has been sexually abused

When confronted with the knowledge, suspicion or allegation of sexual abuse, parents, carers, family members, as well the community (including the church community), have an immediate judgement to make. This judgement will be coloured by such things as past experience and knowledge of the people concerned. It will result in either immediate action to confront the offence or various forms of denial of the offence.

In confronting the offence there are two points of focus both eliciting strong emotions. There is likely to be anger, disgust and possibly fear. While these emotions are in play they are in conflict with and may prevent the therapeutic expression of emotions such as sadness, sympathy, empathy or loving care towards the abused person.

If the response is one of denial (and there are many reasons for denial, such as fear of the abuser, fear of the potential wider consequences, or personal prejudice), then no proper care can be given to the person who has been abused. As explained elsewhere this can then exacerbate the hurt already caused. On the other hand, if the hearer believes that the abuse has occurred but fails to confront it, he or she may personally assume blame or guilt for not preventing the abuse. Essentially those in contact are in the same process as described in the 'Processing abuse' diagram (Figure 1, p. 48) and have decisions to make concerning their emotional survival in the face of denial of the abuse or lack of appropriate action.

Effects on the person who has committed sexual abuse

While this is not the main focus of this section of the report it is relevant to point out that those who commit sexual abuse also are affected emotionally and psychologically by their actions. The processes of handling these consequences are exactly the same as for the person who has been abused or the third parties caught up in events.

The person who has committed sexual abuse can remain in absolute denial of any harm done to their victim and in complete acceptance and justification of his or her own behaviour. He or she also has to direct the resulting suppressed emotional energy (which would otherwise have its healthy expression in guilt, shame, sadness, grief and remorse) to the mechanisms of surviving with denial. This may well include the pursuit of intricate methods of rationalization and justification. Until there has been proper acknowledgement, the person who has abused will remain trapped in the process.

Effects on others in contact with a person who has committed sexual abuse

Each individual response will be based on factors such as past experience and knowledge of the person alleged or proven to have caused sexual abuse. A person's attitudes towards the subject of sexual abuse will also affect their response. If abuse has occurred the consequences are unavoidable even if one of the consequences is avoidance (an aspect of denial). Therefore, the psychological and emotional work of considering aspects of responsibility and the allocation of guilt and the experience of anger or shame, respectively, will be done, consciously or unconsciously. Subsequent behaviour reveals one's judgements of the events. Again, where the person is not wholly convinced of their own integrity in reaching their conclusions, fresh solutions will be sought to quell doubts.

Handling bad news and responding well to stories that are hard to tell

Painful as the processes of handling bad news may be, the way in which third parties cope with it is not just a matter for their own health. It has a profound effect on the outcomes for the person committing the abuse and, more seriously, the person who has been sexually abused.

In order for someone who has survived sexual abuse in the past to tell another person their story, they will need an environment of safety. The death of an offender may provide the 'freedom' to tell. Moving to another country or geographical area, finding safety in a survivors' group or a climate of openness may be other factors that help a person who has experienced abuse to tell their story.

Telling their story calls for enormous courage and a high level of trust. Since it is the nature of abuse to destroy or at least damage trust, it is imperative that when a survivor is ready to tell their story the listener must respond with great sensitivity and care.

Some examples from experience

The following vignettes describe real situations of abuse and a range of responses that have been made. Each is a mixture of cases in order to ensure the protection of those who have found the courage to tell. However, they show the common themes that have been spoken about to Christian Survivors of Sexual Abuse (CSSA) by women and men who asked for help. The responses reported here are followed by a commentary to show what was particularly unhelpful and what would be a more a helpful response. Names that are used do not relate to any real person either alive or dead.

April's Story

April is 46 years old and was sexually abused by her father from age 11 to 14. When she was 14 she ran away from home and was eventually taken into care by social services where she disclosed her abuse. She was fostered for the remainder of her childhood and her father was not prosecuted because she was deemed to be too 'disturbed' to give evidence. Her sisters were subsequently abused. Now she is a practising Roman Catholic Christian and still feels a great deal of shame about what happened to her. She feels that the fact her virginity was lost means she has sinned. She is also concerned that her anger is not suitable in a Christian and this worries her. She further blames herself for leaving her sisters in her father's care and feels guilty that they too were abused. She goes to see a Roman Catholic priest for reassurance in the hope that he can help her deal with some of these issues.

The response April experienced

Fr C is a priest aged 65 belonging to a religious order. He resides in a large religious community and is a well-respected Spiritual Director and many seek his help. At first unable to tell Fr C the real reason she was so angry, April prefers to discuss 'anger' as a general subject in relation to Christianity. This being her first meeting she feels this might be 'safe ground'.

However, Fr C insists that she tell him why she is angry. April prevaricates. She says, 'Something happened in my family home.' Fr C presses further, asking, 'What? I need to know.' Now April feels trapped, and blurts out, 'I was sexually abused by my father.' Fr C then asks her whether she is a virgin. She is shocked and mutters, 'Does that matter?' Fr C replies, 'Yes and no.' This is acutely confusing and April suspects that this has something to do with virginity and the 'no sex before marriage' rules within Christianity. She feels guilt welling up. She does not enlighten Fr C but begins to cry. Fr C says that she should really get herself sorted out psychologically before seeking spiritual help and he advises her to go to confession, 'to confess your sins against impurity'.

April is appalled and leaves the monastery emotionally in shreds. She vows never to speak about it again to a Church person and feels that since this has been so awful maybe there will never be a chance to talk about it.

Commentary on the response April experienced

Fr C came from an era and culture when such issues of child sexual abuse were not well understood. Nevertheless his response is not unusual. The suggestion that virginity is paramount leaves survivors who have been penetrated with special guilt and he has suggested that by telling her to go to confession he has made the right response! In some other Christian traditions April might have been told that she had been spiritually contaminated and would need 'special ministry' (see Rachel's story below).

Fr C also implied April's being upset and crying indicated 'mental illness' and this being so she should not seek spiritual direction as if spiritual direction is not possible for one who is mentally ill – which April clearly is not.

A better response for April

Fr C immediately picks up that April is concerned about anger and discusses with her the fact that Jesus showed anger in the Temple and on other occasions. This meant that to be angry was not a sin but often a natural response to unfair or unjust situations. He asks why she is angry but notices that April is unable to say.

He tells her gently that perhaps she has been badly hurt and it's difficult to talk about. That's fine with him, he doesn't need to know and will always be ready to listen whenever she feels able to tell him more. April feels heartened by Fr C's care of her and decides perhaps she can tell him and just blurts out, 'Dad abused me as a child'. Fr C is shocked and anxious but knows he must have strength for April and says, 'That must have been dreadful'. He asks her if she has been able to seek anyone to talk to, someone who might know about these issues because he admits that he is not a specialist in this area. April says she doesn't know anyone and Fr C says he could try and find someone. April tells him that would be good and feels at last she has a support person.

It is enough for her right now and Fr C simply tells her that the abuse was not her fault even though she might feel it, that she has not sinned and that God loves her. He clearly tells her that anger is a right response and that although he cannot counsel her, for he is not a trained counsellor in this area, he does care that she should feel that he will be with her on her journey of healing.

Fr C and April agree that perhaps they could talk more about her spiritual life and how that has been affected by abuse but that he should help her find a counsellor to talk about the abuse issues. April leaves feeling more supported, that it was OK telling Fr C about her abuse, and is surprised she coped so well. Fr C decides he needs to know more about child sexual abuse as it relates to adults and contacts his diocesan child protection advisor about this. He does not betray April's confidence. He also feels he may need supervision when helping adults in April's situation and makes the appropriate enquiries within his Church.

Commentary on a better response for April

In this version Fr C knows instinctively, through experience, that April has a worrying issue she finds it hard to speak about. So he concentrates on a neutral but relevant subject: anger. When April notes that he is not pressurizing her she relaxes and begins to trust. (This doesn't often happen quite so quickly!) When Fr C hears April tell him of her father, though he feels a natural revulsion and shock, he equally knows he must respond neutrally. His response, 'That must have been dreadful' showed simply that it was wrong and painful for her. He also impresses upon April it was not her fault and she has not sinned.

These messages may need to be heard repeatedly over time. The fact he kept calm helps April to feel he can cope. If he had become upset, judgemental, angry or showed any other strong emotion then April might have become frightened. When April gets to know Fr C he may then tell April how angry he is about it, but the first meeting must be calm.

Fr C is honest: 'That is not my area of expertise, I'm not a counsellor.' This way April knows where she stands, boundaries about what she can expect from him are becoming fixed. However he won't leave her adrift on abuse issues and offers to find a counsellor and to be there for her.

If April had said she didn't need counselling Fr C should continue to maintain he is not a counsellor and cannot offer this. It is important that April knows that although priests and ministers can be supporters that they should not do counselling if they are not trained to do so. Furthermore he recognizes his limitations, seeks advice without naming April and asks for supervision. These are entirely appropriate professional steps because listening well to a survivor of abuse requires this measure of preparation and support.

What Fr C may need to ascertain is where April's father is currently living as he may be a man coming to Mass on Sundays in his parish and steps may need to be taken to protect others. If this were the case then it would be appropriate for the priest to approach diocesan child protection advisers for help in ensuring April's father does not have access to children and is supervised when he comes to Mass. The sharing of this information with the diocesan child protection adviser will need to be first discussed with April, as Fr C will be most anxious to guard her confidentiality. However if he believes there is significant risk to children in his parish this overrides her need for confidentiality. If he must proceed without her permission he must arrange help or support for April as she may still be in great fear of her father.

Rachel's story

Rachel is 25 years old, attends a Pentecostal Church and is a committed Christian. She has suffered depression for years following serious sexual assaults by a teacher in school over a period of time beginning when she was ten years old. While Rachel was still young her abuser was charged and found guilty of numerous sexual offences against six girls in her school. She had to give evidence, which she found traumatic.

What has been difficult for Rachel is that when she told her parents, who were also committed Pentecostal Christians, they told her she had sinned and brought her to church for 'forgiveness and healing'. During this process she was also urged to forgive her abuser. Rachel did as she was asked but for years she has known that this was pretence and she was in fact violently angry with her abuser and does not want to forgive him at all. This has led to feelings of guilt which she finds plunge her into the deepest depression at times. She has asked her friends in church to pray over her for healing of the depression but nothing has happened. Her friends in church told her that she must be 'blocking this healing by some sin'. She believes now that the 'sin' is not forgiving the man who abused her. She arranges to meet with a pastor from another Pentecostal Church to seek his help.

The response Rachel experienced

Rachel knows this pastor a little, but just in passing from some inter-church meetings. He seems to her to be friendly and approachable. She tells him that what she wants to talk about is difficult but then decides directly plunging in would be best. 'Pastor, I was sexually abused when I was ten by the class teacher,' she says, 'and I find I cannot, just cannot forgive him and this worries me, as I am a Christian. What must I do to forgive?'

The pastor tells Rachel that the Lord asks that we forgive everyone as he forgives us. That Jesus said we must forgive seventy times seven. Not to forgive would indeed be sinful. He asks whether Rachel has prayed for the 'gift of forgiveness'. Rachel says that she has.

The pastor then suggests that perhaps something evil has entered her through her experience that is hindering her from forgiving. He tells her he will arrange for special ministry next Sunday and that she should fast during the week with only one small meal a day. Rachel is very scared but she desperately hates her inner turmoil and thinks that this might just work.

On the day in question Rachel is quite weak from lack of food. She is put into the middle of a circle of worshippers who are holding hands. They begin to pray fervently in English and in tongues; some shouting loudly that the devil should leave her. Some lay hands on her and some actually hit her to 'drive the evil from her'. In the midst of this she starts to panic and feels utterly trapped. This trapped sensation reminds her of being with the teacher and she has severe flashbacks. She tries to escape the circle but cannot. She ends up in a foetal position on the floor. It is only then that the group leave her as they feel she needs to be 'alone'. She finally unwinds enough to get home. On Monday morning she takes an overdose and ends up in hospital.

Commentary on the response Rachel experienced

Forgiveness is discussed in Chapter 11 of this Report. It has been found to be the most difficult Christian issue for those who have survived sexual abuse. It is often totally misunderstood by both lay people and clergy. Rachel had come to believe that her depression is a direct result of not forgiving, but this is not necessarily the case, as we shall see in the next response to Rachel. The pastor she consulted tried to impose his own view of healing without ascertaining whether Rachel is psychologically or emotionally able or stable enough to undergo such a publicly humiliating event. He failed to understand the necessity for Rachel to feel in control after a long period without control when she was abused.

Effectively those within her church were blaming Rachel and this compounded her guilt and depression. Though she appeared willing to try anything to 'feel better' she has not anticipated that it could trigger panics and flashbacks. The pastor, had he understood the dynamics of panic attacks and flashbacks that are common to those who survive sexual abuse, may have reconsidered the format of 'ministry' arranged for her. He had focused exclusively on a spiritual course of action when he ought to have considered what is required psychologically and emotionally as well.

Within any pastoral situation there is always a duty of care. A competent pastor should recognize signs of emotional distress and the consequences of trauma, and therefore take great care not to exacerbate these. A more careful, informed and considered approach was required.

A better response to Rachel

Rachel is in hospital recovering from her overdose. She refuses to talk to the male psychiatrist because she feels he would never understand. However the hospital has a female chaplain who comes onto the ward and Rachel spots her. She asks to talk with her. The chaplain (also a Pentecostal) has vast experience of pastoral care, and had worked for a year at a local refuge for women escaping domestic abuse where she had spoken to many women about their childhood experiences. Following that she did a counselling diploma and is a qualified counsellor.

Rachel tells her story including what had happened in the church and how frightened, controlled and humiliated she felt. She fears God's wrath and she fears just about everything but is desperate to be 'better'.

The chaplain asks Rachel what she means exactly by 'forgiving her abuser'. Rachel suddenly realizes she has not thought about this properly before. This is a bit of a revelation! Recognizing this the chaplain then suggests that perhaps Rachel's confusion and her inability to understand clearly what she thinks forgiveness means is probably because she's never discussed or explored her past experience. She reassures Rachel that God is not going to condemn her for not forgiving, as God knows that in her heart she is striving for this. Equally God knows all that Rachel has experienced and that her journey will take twists and turns. She tells Rachel that God is gentle and gives her time. There is no pressure. God is telling Rachel to care for herself first and to come to these issues slowly and carefully.

The chaplain tells her that she would like to hear more about Rachel's past before discussing forgiveness and asks her how she felt about being abused, how she felt about her parents' response, how she felt about going to court, how she feels right now. She arranges a series of meetings with Rachel and tells her they will work on these things first.

Over the course of the meetings and by concentrating on Rachel's feelings, the chaplain helps Rachel to see that a great deal needs to be explored in therapy before she can finally think about 'forgiveness'. Rachel realizes she has never had the chance to talk about what happened and that until she sorts out all these things and understands that none of it was her fault she cannot move on to deal with the spiritual bits.

Rachel has also learned that much of her depression is due to her unresolved feelings about abuse, not about her lack of forgiveness, though she still wants to look at that when the time is right. She now recognizes that some therapy and counselling will have to come first.

Commentary on a better response for Rachel

The chaplain realized quickly that at an inappropriately young age Rachel had been pressured to 'forgive' without the maturity to understand this. It was this that had created an unhealthy and unhelpful understanding of 'forgiveness'. Rachel was still locked into a child's understanding of forgiveness. In order for Rachel to approach forgiveness with a mature perspective her perception as a child and her adult understanding of what happened to her must first be addressed. Asking a survivor to forgive before he or she has had this chance is dangerous and confusing. Furthermore the chaplain knows that Rachel needs less pressure to forgive in order to give her space to be who she is and explore her past. The chaplain knows that Rachel does not need more pressure but the freedom to explore. This she should do with a qualified counsellor or therapist.

John's story

John is 56 years old. He was only 12 when his older brother of 24 began to molest him sexually and raped him. He subsequently found out that his father had sexually abused his older brother when he was a child. John is a committed Christian. He has never spoken about his past, though members of his church do know it was not a happy childhood. He is married with three lovely children and he is trying to provide the sort of home that he never had when he was growing up.

His wife knows about his abuse and is able to reassure him about her love for him. He is the churchwarden and a member of the Parochial Church Council (PCC). His church has *produced a Child Protection Policy and the PCC feels that the church members must have training for protecting children and in how to deal with disclosures. They are committed to making the church a safe place.*

John is asked to find out who might offer this training and to look at various materials that might be useful. John would like to tell the PCC that this would be difficult for him because of his past, but he is afraid to tell them. At home he discusses this with his wife and she encourages him to try to tell his fellow PCC members. But when he does so, the other members are aghast at John's disclosure and no one makes any response whatsoever, preferring to change the subject and move on to the next item on the agenda.

John feels rejected and unheard, and a feeling of 'I should never have told' seeps into his mind. He goes home desperately depressed and does not share this with his wife. He does decide he will have to talk with the vicar.

The response John experienced

John determines that when he meets with the vicar privately he will tell him that he was not happy with the PCC's response, and arranges a meeting in a week's time. The vicar receives John cautiously. He seems nervous and distant. John explains that he was shocked at the way his fellow PCC members had ignored his disclosure and that he felt unsupported by the PCC. He wants to be reassured that the vicar will offer some measure of support and be proactive at the PCC meeting in generating a better response towards him.

The vicar tells John that he is glad that he has come to speak to him as there are number of things that he wants to discuss with John. He is sorry about John's past experiences but it leaves him in a dilemma. The vicar then tells John that he would like him to relinquish his leadership of the Bible study with the teenage children, as it might prove difficult for John. When John asks why this sudden decision and what exactly he means by 'might be difficult for him', the vicar rather anxiously tells him that several parents on hearing of John's background feel John may not be safe with children. After all, they conclude, if you have been abused you may go on to abuse. John is totally outraged and storms out of the vicarage tremendously upset.

Commentary on the response John experienced

John feels his position within his church community is now seriously at risk and the fact that the vicar has accepted stereotypes is profoundly worrying for him. The vicar appears to be ignoring John's feelings and compounds his sense of rejection by asking him to relinquish his job as Bible study leader with the teenagers. John starts to feel like a sex offender! The vicar presents his request to John in the guise of a child protection action, when in fact it appears more likely that the vicar is concerned to keep other parishioners happy at John's expense.

John feels so profoundly wounded that he cannot speak to his wife and his depression and hurt grow without the benefit of an objective 'outsider' to help to provide a sense of perspective. John becomes angry and irritable and his family suffers. He feels he will have to leave the church and decides if he does then he will leave God as well, as the hypocrisy of Christianity seems to shine through right now!

A better response for John

After the PCC meeting the vicar rings up a child protection worker he knows and asks whether there is any material that he could read about supporting male survivors of sexual abuse. He then buys two recommended books. Meanwhile parishioners have started a 'whispering' campaign, which is turning nasty, and the vicar wants this 'nipped in the bud' quickly. He seeks advice on how to counter the parishioners' negative assumptions about John from the child protection worker.

When John comes to see him, the vicar says that he is glad John came, as the information he gave the PCC was very shocking and he wants to know from John how he might support him. John says that he was stunned by the lack of warm response and the vicar suggests that this truly indicated that a training course was paramount and that their poor response was probably a result of ignorance. He tells John that he is glad he was so honest as he felt keeping such secrets must be intolerable. He adds that he feels sure that other male survivors will be encouraged by John's openness and honesty and only good can come eventually from such openness.

He shares with John that some parishioners are saying John could be a sex offender and warns John that he may be met with caution and hostility. However he intends to speak to the main protagonists and tell them that he is not happy with their derogatory assumptions. He suggests John and he will ride this storm together and quickly get the child protection programme up and running. Meanwhile if John could continue in his role as Bible study leader he'd be very grateful, though he knows this might be difficult for him.

As a further act of support he asks whether John would like to discuss his past with the child protection worker, if only to see how he can cope with the parish's response. He also tells John that talking to his wife (he knows John didn't do that) would be helpful and advises John that he needs someone 'outside of himself' to be a sounding board and support.

John thinks all these suggestions are good ones and will act on them. He leaves with a firm sense that his vicar supports him. He is relieved and grateful. He resolves to hold on to the fact he knows he is not an abuser and that ignorance is at the bottom of these negative reactions. He knows it will be a tough time and only with training might his parish understand male survivors.

Commentary on a better response for John

The assumption that an abused person will automatically become an abuser is a common assumption which is erroneous and can be very damaging. The vicar's good response in this illustration is everything that is required. Training for all church members is vitally important if survivors are not to be victimized within a society where parents become ever more frightened for their children. Such training is commonly available within most denominational structures, but there are other outside bodies that can also help.

Meena's story

Meena is Asian and 22 years old. She grew up in care in England and became a Christian when she was 15. She attends a local church.

When she was eight years old her foster father sexually abused Meena. The abuse went on for two years before she could tell anyone, and she was removed and placed in another family. Subsequently she has always found sex and sexuality issues impossible to deal with and as a consequence does not have boyfriends, or indeed many friends at all as the abuse she suffered makes it difficult to enter into relationships of trust.

Her minister notices how isolated Meena is and suggests she come to him for counselling. Meena agrees as she likes her minister and she is very lonely. She tells him about her background and he says he can help. However she must be prepared to talk about her past, including about sex and sexuality. He says that these are gifts from God and that she should learn to accept these gifts. He will help her.

The response Meena experienced

The minister spends many weeks talking with Meena on safe and neutral topics. Gradually he introduces the topic of sex and sexuality. He feels that as a 'holy' minister he could help Meena experience a 'good and healthy' relationship. He suggests at first that he hugs Meena. She is not that keen but feels that a hug should be all right so agrees. Several weeks later he kisses her on the forehead and Meena again interprets this as a friendly kiss and that becoming comfortable with it will teach her to become closer to men. The minister is always gentle, always kind and this is exactly what Meena needs. She has never been shown affection.

One day he kisses Meena on the lips and fondles her breasts and genitals. He stops and tells Meena, 'You liked that because you responded and let me do it, you are improving.' Meena is totally confused. On the one hand she is beginning to like touch; on the other hand she is not sure if this is OK. She is also very confused because she knows her minister would not hurt her and that this is sexual education by which she should be learning how to accept God's gift of sex and sexuality. She feels he must know what he is doing as he is a man of God. On the other hand there are doubts creeping in and she's becoming a bit afraid and ashamed.

Commentary on the response Meena experienced

Meena is a vulnerable young woman. She grew up in care and was sexually abused. She comes from an ethnic minority and may feel excluded and isolated within the community. She may not have relatives to turn to and we know she has few friends. Meena is not comfortable discussing sex and sexuality and has openly said this to him. He knows her vulnerabilities, he knows her loneliness, and he knows her fears. He is also in a powerful position as a white male professional pastor. He has exploited Meena's position and uses her for his own sexual gratification.

Although he has tried to justify his behaviour as a sort of healing/educative method, he has sexually abused her. He has exploited Meena's inability to form relationships, and exploited her naïvety. Meena will not gain from this experience. Indeed she will be further damaged.

A better response for Meena

The minister notices Meena's loneliness and lack of friends. He invites her to come and see him in a safe environment; she does so, partly because he asks, partly because he's a nice man. Meena tells him she finds it difficult to trust people after being in care and being abused. He tells her one of these situations alone would have been enough to knock her confidence and trust in people. He tries to discover whom she has in her life who supports her. He discovers her foster mother was very good to her and is still in contact and supporting her. She also has a college tutor with whom she talks and who knows her background. Having established that she has a small network of support, he asks her if she has ever had counselling and she says no.

He discusses this with her and says that he could try and find a counsellor for her or perhaps her college has one. Meena says she has been too nervous to go to counselling. The minister reminds her that the church fellowship will always be there for her and suggests she arranges one appointment and then comes back to him and tell him how it went (but not the content of her counselling session). Meena decides with this support she will try just one session. He says that this is a start and to take it one step at a time. He says, 'Counselling might help you to trust more and be less lonely.'

Commentary on a better response for Meena

The minister has suggested to Meena that counselling might be helpful but only after he checks to see if she has a network of support as counselling might bring up difficult issues and he wants to know that she has someone to turn to if necessary. However counselling could still be offered even if Meena did not have a supportive network. He could try to help Meena build up her support network within the church fellowship, being sure to pick trustworthy people to help her, at first perhaps women only because of her past experience. He recognizes and keeps his boundaries. He is not a counsellor; he is not skilled in responding to sexual abuse issues. He does not hug her or kiss her or hold her hand, recognizing that such touch might pitch her back into abuse memories that could be harmful. In any case he feels it would be inappropriate to do so.

Conclusions

As already stated, these vignettes are a compilation of a range of actual situations known to the Working Group. They are neither uncommon nor extreme examples. Inappropriate responses are all too common within churches across the denominational spectrum.

It is vital our churches are safe places for people to tell their stories of abuse, and where people listen and respond well. Knowledge about child sexual abuse is really helpful but most of all survivors want honesty. It is quite all right to say that stories of sexual abuse are distressing, difficult to listen to and to discuss. Even if a hearer has to say it hurts them so badly they are not really the right person for the survivor to talk to, even this will be understood. Survivors know it is a difficult discussion topic. However a refusal to engage in the issues may be perceived as evasive and hurtful to survivors who often feel that they have had to deal with the pain, and the least a Christian sister or brother could do is to try! Rejection, avoidance, or telling a survivor to 'forgive and forget' almost always compounds the existing hurt, increases shame and guilt and is a failure to show true Christian love.

CHAPTER SEVEN

Ripples in a pond

Elaine's story

Elaine is 22 years old, living with her parents and young sister, aged 14 years. Mother, father and daughters attend a local church regularly. Father takes a lead in youth work for the church.

The family is puzzled and hurt because Elaine has pulled out of the relationship with Mark, whom she was planning to marry, and will give no reason. Mark's and Elaine's extended family are very upset and angry.

Finally, Elaine begins to talk to her aunt to whom she has always been close. She tells her aunt that she cannot enter into a sexual relationship with Mark because of the sexual abuse she experienced when she was 14 years old. Finally, with great distress she discloses that the offender was the vicar and that the grooming and the abuse that continued over six months occurred when she stayed behind after youth club to help clear up the hall. Elaine felt quite unable to tell anyone at the time because this vicar was so loved and admired by everyone and she felt she would not be believed.

When her secret is shared and Elaine agrees to go to the police, her mother, father and close family do not believe her and the family becomes very distraught. Mark and his family want to go to the neighbouring parish to beat up the vicar, especially after they hear him deny the offences in court.

The disclosure means that the social services and police question youth workers and young people in the vicar's present parish as well as the friends of Elaine who had attended the youth club.

The parish splits into people who believe Elaine and those who blame her and her family for destroying the vicar's ministry and care by sending him to prison.

*When Elaine's secret is told, she is left unsupported and alone
– her future marriage unlikely to happen. She needs
therapeutic help to allow her to come to terms with the abuse
and her future close relationships, but this is not available.*

*The congregations of both churches are split, hurt and unable
to support each other, let alone respond appropriately to the
victim and her fiancé. Sadly, although the immediate family
are leading members of the church, there is not enough
understanding and experience within the church to help them
work through their feelings of failure, anger and distress.*

The effects of abuse and of its disclosure are far-reaching. There
are implications not just for the person who has experienced abuse
and the person who has abused, but for their families and
friends, for groups and networks of which they are part, and for the
wider community.

The destructive nature of abuse within society is exacerbated when
it involves the faith community, because the element of trust is
destroyed, not only in an individual – be it clergy or lay – but in the
institution of the Church which is built on the premise of love and care
shown by Christ as its head and cornerstone.

Within the Christian community, therefore, even the possibility of
abuse of children, young people and vulnerable adults is often
unrecognized or met with disbelief and horror. It has been shown by
research that contrary to media coverage which promotes the view that
sex offenders are strangers or part of networks in the public arena, the
majority of sexual abuse takes place within relationships within
families or social networks. This again challenges church members
where the concept of family is so important.

The invasion of family networks by the abuser is far-reaching. In
order to remain undetected the abuser grooms potential victims and
therefore damages relationships between parents and children, work
colleagues or neighbours and friends. In other words the whole
network of family and congregation becomes involved and
relationships distorted. Once the offence is disclosed these networks
feel tainted and may collude to avoid guilt or rejection. Christian
communities often have a very real need to retain their inner trust and
so they are often led to deny wickedness in their midst and will be less
than willing to hear the victim's story objectively, or recognize the pain
that an abuser spreads in wider and wider circles like ripples in a pond.

Everyone is part of a number of networks, so as well as the
complex psychological responses of the victim, there are the responses

of those within networks. The variation in response, sometimes quite hurtful to the victim, leads to a further set of feelings to be understood and responded to. Although victims do not appear to be isolated, many keep their abuse secret often for many years, through fear, guilt, coercion and in some cases ignorance and naïvety. When the situation is eventually disclosed and is no longer secret, there is often misunderstanding, disbelief and failure to acknowledge the suffering.

It is often asked, 'Why has it been so long a secret? Why did you not tell your partner at the time of marriage? Was anyone else in the family aware? Was there anyone else being abused?' If the failure to disclose until much later in life has led to dysfunction and flawed relationships then the reasons for disclosure may be misunderstood. It is important to understand that there may be people who will have lived and shared closely in the lives of the victims without recognizing there was anything amiss. Often, these same people have blamed the victim because their response and behaviour was unacceptable and could not be understood.

When abuse is in the family context it is often felt by victims and other family members that the 'secret' is best kept, because disclosure could lead to the 'blowing apart' of the family. The consequences of that can be used as a means of preserving the secret and protecting the 'greater good'. For example, when the secret is disclosed, the family may cling to the secret rather than risk a loved father going to prison or siblings being taken into care, which may be part of the process. This leads to secondary abuse involving the networks in the nuclear and extended family. The maintenance of this secret is frequently undermined when another abused person discloses and investigations are started and the protective network of the family collapses in disarray and despair. The same processes are often at work in the 'family' of the church.

It is these pressures which often prevent the victim from sharing – fearing they will destroy their family and their faith network and believing it is better to suffer in secret. It is during this stage of secrecy that significant behaviour changes may occur in the victim's personality, leading many people to criticize and reject them and the victim is less likely to be heard sympathetically. However telling the story can be healing for some victims when it is handled sensitively and its power should not be underestimated. We need to remember that the repeated telling of the story, as in bereavement or separation, is a normal part of the healing process, even if the listeners find the repetition difficult and ask, 'Why do they keep going on about it? Why don't they put it behind them?'

Once the secret is told there are very many varied responses from within the family (nuclear and extended), wider community, school, work, social networks and Christian community. These encompass disbelief, denial, extreme anger, sympathy, guilt at failure to protect or complete dissociation. All of these will be experienced by the perpetrator and their family as well as the victim and their family.

At this time the police and social services may be investigating the allegation. Frequently, the length of investigation also leads to huge stress on the victim and their family, because the collection of evidence requires yet more secrecy and restrictions in order not to distort the evidence, which might prevent a criminal prosecution. These restrictions will affect all efforts to support the victim. Inner circles can be so devastated by disclosure or discovery that any obvious support structures are unable to function because of their own distress. Outer circles are also prevented by restrictions in the legal process from offering support at the most important time. There is not even the offer of therapy for the victim until after the court case, although this is now being challenged.

If legal proceedings are invoked there is a further process of difficult experiences for the victim and their family and close associates. This will include the local church congregation, who will experience similar emotional responses of a complex nature, to those of the family. Some will believe the story, some will reject it outright, some will find their faith is challenged. Some will respond with extreme anger bordering on violence. Untold harm can be the result of this broken trust so important to the integrity of the Christian community.

Statistics indicate that only a small percentage of allegations lead to prosecutions and an even smaller percentage of convictions are achieved. The criminal justice system is adversarial and evidential and victims subject to this process suffer again; so many refuse to allow their cases to enter the process. It may be that a process of civil law would be a more appropriate avenue where the balance of probability instead of proof beyond reasonable doubt is more sensitive to the nuances of sexual abuse cases, and therefore not as damaging to the victims. It should not be overlooked that being part of a criminal process revisits in public the pain and hurt of the actual abuse and if prosecution is not successful it does not allow the therapeutic healing of justice to be achieved. The interest of the media in a court case can be highly damaging because a much wider audience will often receive a partial or sometimes incorrect report. It is at this stage that the wider network of the victim and their family, such as school, work and leisure will react to the situation appropriately or inappropriately.

In view of the complexities outlined above, how can the Church offer a safe and accepting place where judgement will not be made? If the abuse has been within the congregation or ministry it has to be recognized that church members may not be acceptable as pastoral carers; but that there is a responsibility to ensure that support and pastoral care is available from another source. Most churches do not have appropriately trained persons to undertake counselling in sexual abuse but should always be able to refer the victim to the appropriate organizations for help.

When working with these situations there is a need to recognize the possibility of reawakening personal abusive experiences within the listeners, which may evoke an unexpected response such as 'I cannot talk or help with this situation at the moment because it brings back too many painful memories'. The ripples spreading from one person's story affect the pastoral care and what can be offered within the church. The pastor has to be a facilitator of interventions, which need to be offered at different levels by a variety of carers. It is also absolutely essential that the pastor is not seen to be taking sides. In particular, it is inappropriate for the same person to seek to offer pastoral support both to the person who has experienced abuse and the person who has abused.

It is only in recent years the taboo of speaking of sexual behaviour has been lifted and it has become possible to talk of sexual abuse. Until now the Church has not taken a lead in providing a safe place for disclosure, in fact many who may have tried to talk about their abuse within the Church have suffered further abuse because their story has been unacceptable. In some cases victims as well as perpetrators have been advised to move elsewhere, thereby allowing the church community to avoid scandal. In the future our hope is that the Christian community will learn to become a safe, loving and healing environment to allow the process of disclosure to go on amongst its members and those outside whom the Church seeks to serve.

We must not ignore the fact that the Church could lead the way in society for the provision of a safe, confidential place, where people with painful stories can be heard and supported on their journey to justice and healing. In order to work towards this each church should include within its code of practice a statement to ensure that victims can and will be heard and that within their Christian community there is an appropriate person to whom they can be referred.

Some readers of *Time for Action* are likely to say that the Church already is precisely the kind of safe, confidential place described in the previous paragraph. This may often be the case. Unfortunately, the experiences that led to the writing of *The Courage to Tell* and *Time for Action* demonstrate that at other times the Church, and those who represent it, have not been experienced as safe. At times, people have tried to tell their story but not been listened to. People have come seeking help and have been abused by a person appointed by the Church to offer pastoral care.

CHAPTER EIGHT

Abuse of adults within the Church

In addition to clergy and ministers, who are specially trained to offer pastoral care, there are many people in a church who may become involved in it. They may be lay people who offer services such as 'healing ministry' or prayer support. There are those involved in working with children and young people, or in spiritual direction and leading retreats. There are religious sisters and brothers who have a role and service within the church. And there are people who are not the pastor of the church but have other roles, such as elder, steward or churchwarden.

Both ordained and non-ordained people who engage in pastoral care and who have pastoral responsibility have a responsibility to engage in ethical and sound relationships with the persons they are supporting. Guidelines are required for all those who are caring for vulnerable people within congregations and communities.

When considering sexual exploitation and the violation of pastoral care relationships, it is clear that those who perpetrate abuse may be lay people, religious or ordained minister. The major focus of this chapter, however, is on those involved in ordained ministries though churches that have no ordained ministry and individuals who are not ordained but who are involved in offering pastoral care will find much that is written here relates equally to their situation. For clarity the word 'minister' (rather than 'priest', 'pastor', etc.) is used throughout this chapter.

Ordained ministers are specifically charged with a duty of care. They have inordinate power over lay people due to their role, ministry and position of trust. Ministers have been taken into a special closeness and given privileged access and knowledge by people in their congregations and communities normally afforded only to intimate friends. Another factor of importance is the power of the minister's *office* within a specific *value system*. This chapter, therefore, looks at this specific and special relationship and the sexual boundary violations that have occurred with survivors of sexual abuse who have turned to ministers for help and support.

The Conference of Religious in Ireland recently produced a booklet, *Ministry with Integrity, a Consultation Document about Standards in Pastoral Ministry.*[1] This lays out an ethical framework for pastoral care and covers issues such as boundaries, power, accountability, confidentiality, dual-relationships and transference and counter-transference. The Group also had sight of a leaflet produced by Ministers and Clergy Sexual Abuse Survivors MACSAS, *Clergy or Minister Sexual Exploitation of Adults in the Pastoral Relationship.*[2] This offers guidance on the limits and boundaries of the pastoral relationship. We also drew upon the work of one of the members who is undertaking her PhD on 'clergy sexual exploitation of women in the pastoral relationship' and on her experience in interviewing many women so exploited.

Three cases of sexual exploitation within the church known to the Group

Case one

A woman in her twenties sought the help of a minister of a house church who was in his fifties. Originally she saw him individually over some spiritual difficulties she was having. Several people had sexually abused this young woman as a child and although she told her minister about this and he said that nothing like this would happen between them, it did. She was unable to deal effectively with sexual behaviour. He had given her all sorts of scriptural reasons as to why it was his duty to engage her sexually and told her that 'concubines were biblical'. After about eight years she realized that several other young women went for counselling after his abuse of them and that she was not the only one. She felt foolish, victimized, abused, used and outraged. She says that she was vulnerable and that he saw that she did not have boundaries as her previous abusers had taken these away.

Case two

A woman who had previously had two periods in a psychiatric hospital for depression and had been sexually abused as a child was in college trying to rebuild a career after her first chosen career collapsed because of a physical impairment. She was still very depressed and saw the college counsellor every week, if not twice a week. She also attended the Christian Union, where she met the college chaplain. He was caring and supportive and she welcomed, at first, his warmth and nurturing. She often called him to her flat when she was desperate, drunk or had overdosed and he often came to take her to hospital. He began to abuse her sexually when she was in one of these very distressed states. For several months she could not tell anyone until he took her one day to a forest and seriously sexually assaulted her. Then she told her counsellor who warned the chaplain away from her. He left the country. Years later she went to the country where he was living and with a therapist confronted him. He apologized and admitted he'd planned the sexual involvement and that she was not the only one. His bishop removed him from full ministry, though he is still allowed to preach.

Case three

A young woman of twenty, who was in the care of psychiatric services, got involved with a charismatic group run by the husband of one of her college tutors. She liked the singing and the meeting with young people and was searching for help out of her deep confusion and depression. She was on medication and self-injured on a regular basis. The tutor's husband recommended that she see a 'healing' priest and she did so. On the first meeting he sexually assaulted her whilst chanting and praying and laying hands on her. On a subsequent occasion he did the same. Many years later, on hearing about research into sexual exploitation of adults by ministers and getting involved in that research she decided to report this priest. She received a letter from his provincial that the priest in question had been in a residential therapy centre, twice, to 'modify his ministry'. She was shocked, as this obviously meant other people had similar experiences and had also reported him. She discovered he'd been sent to work in Africa. She worried for the people who would be exposed to his behaviour, probably not knowing his background. Recently she went to the police and reported him.

Are priests and ministers professionals?

There is now growing awareness that professionals such as psychologists, psychiatrists, psychotherapists, nurses, doctors, etc. can and do sometimes sexually exploit their clients. For this reason regulatory bodies have disciplinary procedures and there is access to complaints procedures for clients within those professional ethical guidelines. The issue of whether priests and ministers should be regarded as another 'professional' body is debated within a number of publications.

Richard Gula SS, a professor of moral theology, in *Ethics in Pastoral Ministry*,[3] argues that 'pastoral ministry' is both a vocation and a profession. He defines the two terms thus:

Vocation: . . . a free response to God's call in and through the community to commit oneself in love to serve others. The communal dimension of a vocation means that the call to ministry is heard within the Church, is sustained by the Church, and is to serve the mission of the Church. There is no private, individualistic vocation to ministry.

Profession:. . . . the commitment to acquire expert knowledge and skills and to serve human needs with good moral character . . . The positive meaning of being professional connotes a specialised competence, integrity, selfless dedication to serve the community, and to holding trust.

It is because the pastoral ministry is both vocation and profession that the role of the minister is so powerful. Many people seeking help will be looking for a person in whom they can invest a great deal of trust, whom they perceive as God's representative here on earth and therefore a 'holy' and safe person who has training and skills to help them. The power of the minister is seen as the 'power of God' and a vulnerable person may be looking for that power to influence their life for good. So it is important to look carefully at the pastoral relationships of priests and ministers.

Power

Gula[4] says:

The pastoral relationship is not a peer relationship. Instead it is marked by the power of the pastoral minister and the vulnerability of the one being served . . . In relationships where one party is stronger than the other, or more in control of the encounter, *the greater burden of responsibility lies on the one with the greater power.* (Original emphasis).

Gula seeks to be very clear as to the role and purpose of pastoral ministry particularly when people seek help from a minister. He says:

Our pastoral commitment is to provide a safe place for people to be vulnerable without the fear of being exploited. This means not only that we must not sexualise the pastoral relationship but we must say 'no' to any sexualised behaviour towards us.

Ministry with Integrity considers the 'use of power'[5] and describes the obligations of the pastoral minister in the use of that power. Pastoral ministers are (to be):

- Aware of the unique power that they exercise over those seeking pastoral service, they use that power in ways that respect the dignity of persons, empowering them to exercise their own freedom and so share more fully in the mission of the Church.

- Sufficiently self-disciplined as to maintain clear boundaries in their pastoral relationship and always refrain from exploiting the trust and dependency of those who seek their service, not using them to satisfy their personal needs for attention, acceptance and pleasure.

- Careful to avoid, as far as possible, dual relationships, which would impair personal judgement. They thus avoid conflicts of interest or the exploitation of the pastoral relationship for personal gain.

- Aware that dual relationships are sometimes unavoidable in pastoral ministry, they must lessen the potential for conflicts of interest and exploitation by monitoring the development of the relationship through supervision, peer review and/or spiritual direction.

- Aware of the possible imbalance of power among professional and pastoral colleagues and avoid bullying those who work with them and for whom they work.

Most people seeking help of ministers will perceive the contact as potentially bringing therapeutic, spiritual or personal benefit. They are often in distress, vulnerable, sad, confused or frightened. They may be in great personal difficulties due to marital stress, work problems, problems with children or previous abuse as a child. Therefore, in a sense, they approach ministers from a client role. Although this word is not often used of pastoral relationships it is meaningful in this context. They may also see the minister as 'friend' more than as professional, and ministers often find themselves in such 'dual roles', but this makes it doubly important that the minister should be continually aware of his or her status, power and position as minister. The person in such a role acts as a professional deemed to have skills, expertise and power to effect change in the other person's circumstances. The minister therefore holds the complete responsibility for keeping the boundaries. The minister has always more power than the person seeking help although he or she may not *feel* that this is the case. 'Feelings' are not, however, the barometer of how relationships are to be conducted ethically and professionally. There is always a power differential between the minister and the one seeking help.

Therefore, when a sexual relationship develops within a pastoral relationship this is not an 'affair', but a breach of professional ethical guidelines and a boundary violation. The trust needed to sustain a pastoral relationship has been betrayed and the major responsibility for this is with the minister. *Ministry with Integrity*[6] says, 'because of the inequality of power in the pastoral relationship, the greater burden of responsibility falls on the minister to keep the boundaries clear.'

Boundaries and the keeping of boundaries are important concepts when addressing right relationships within pastoral care.

Boundaries

In her book *At Personal Risk: Boundary Violations in Professional–Client Relationships*[7] Marilyn Peterson comments upon the importance of boundaries. She writes: 'Boundaries protect the space that must exist between professional and client by controlling the power differential in the relationship. They allow for a safe connection based on our needs not on those of the professional.'

The same is true in pastoral relationships. *Ministry with Integrity*[8] has this to say about boundaries in the pastoral relationship:

- Boundary violations are committed when the minister knowingly or unknowingly crosses the emotional, physical, spiritual or sexual limits of another.
- The minister is always responsible for maintaining appropriate behaviour.
- Ministers never initiate sexual behaviour and refuse it when another initiates it.
- Ministers are prudent in physical touch.
- Ministers are familiar themselves with the dynamics of transference and counter-transference and their consequences.
- Ministers always satisfy their needs for affection, intimacy and friendship outside the pastoral relationship.
- Ministers avoid anything in speech or behaviour that might involve sexual harassment of another.
- Ministers choose an appropriate physical environment in which to exercise ministry.

- Ministers are discerning and prudent in showing expressions of regard and in giving and receiving of gifts.
- Where the bond of trust is jeopardized by encroachment on the boundaries, the minister takes steps to bring the relationship to a close and arranges referral to another minister.

In many situations ministers are obliged to balance roles as pastor, priest, professional person and friend. This is true for all churches but perhaps applies particularly to clergy of established or national churches, who have a responsibility for everyone who lives in their parish. It cannot be avoided and is part of their life. It does, however, mean that great care must be taken.

Boundaries within the counselling role

A person seeking help will often speak of the minister as a 'counsellor' whether this be for pastoral counselling or spiritual counselling. Ministers sometimes describe themselves as 'counsellors', even though many have training in pastoral care rather than counselling. The person seeking help is often unaware that the minister they are seeing has no clinical training or expertise in this area, or, indeed, supervision. It is the fact of priesthood/ministry which makes the person seeking help believe the minister has skills, or even that the minister has been invested by God with special powers. It is well known in the counselling/psychological community that clients sometimes invest their counsellors with a special authority. Counsellors occupy a unique position of trust, and can have a tremendous influence on the course of people's lives and close relationships. They can have a major influence on their clients' sense of self-worth in terms of relationships and core values. The sense of power may be greater in clergy pastoral relationships due to the spiritual power of God, which is presumed to be in the hands of the clergy person.

Transference/Counter-transference

Pastoral relationships can be further complicated by the phenomena of transference and counter-transference. 'Transference' is demonstrated when we act towards a person now as if he or she is the same as a significant person from our past. In 'counter-transference' we are in the helper role and our unmet needs and feelings are superimposed upon the person coming for our help.

While this analytical model goes a long way to help us understand some of the exploitation that occurs and how a needy person may seek closeness and how an unaware minister might respond sexually, it does not account for all exploitation scenarios. There are ministers who *intentionally* and *deliberately* sexualize a pastoral relationship and target a vulnerable woman, even when the woman has *not* in any way had a 'transference' response to the minister.

Responding to inappropriate behaviour

When individuals are confronted with inappropriate behaviour on the part of the minister, they may accede or comply because they do not want to lose what is important and valued in the relationship – the valuable part of their experience in the pastoral encounter. This vulnerability to acceding or complying is well understood by professional counsellors and it is their absolute duty not to exploit it. Some people feel 'in love' with the minster giving them pastoral care but this is 'transference love' and is well documented in the writings on therapy and counselling. Vulnerable people who have experienced previous trauma or abusive relationships in the past may not be able to discern an abusive sexual boundary violation by a counsellor or minister and it is such people who are at most risk and are indeed targeted. The minister comes across initially as caring, warm and helpful. In the process of pastoral care the client then feels 'transference love' for their caring minister. When the minister then breaches the sexual boundaries the vulnerable client believes the relationship is a 'love relationship'. It is not.

Many people have difficulty understanding the inability of a person seeking help to protect themselves from exploitative relationships. But the space between professional responsibility and client vulnerability creates fundamental inequalities in terms of who has the power, and diminishes the client's ability to be self-determining.

Victims of abuse experience intensely mixed feelings towards the perpetrators of the abuse, especially in the early stages, which range between affection, appreciation, distrust, confusion and anger. They frequently have a strong sense of responsibility about what has happened to them and fear hurting the perpetrator if they lodge a complaint. They fear reprisal and, unfortunately, this fear is not unfounded. There is obviously great difficulty in integrating such a wide range of conflicting emotions.

Consent

The issue of 'consent' is frequently misunderstood in these relationships. Many organizations and governing bodies argue that these sorts of relationships are between two consenting adults. However, it will be seen from the above that this is not a relationship between two consenting adults. Involvement with a professional is never comparable to an extramarital affair or a love affair. Peter Rutter MD, in his book *Sex in the Forbidden Zone,*[9] suggests:

> sexual behaviour is always wrong, no matter who initiates it, no matter how willing the participants say they are. In the Forbidden Zone factors of power, trust and dependency remove the possibility of the client giving consent to sexual contact. Put another way, the dynamics of the Forbidden Zone can render a client unable to withhold consent. And because the professional has the greater power, the responsibility is his to guard the forbidden boundary against sexual contact.

This also applies to women and men seeking the help of clergy whom they perceive in the role of *professional.*

Compliance should never be confused with consent. Clients who in normal circumstances are totally sensible and could not easily be seduced will accede to sex. Assuming that clients have a choice when embarking on a sexual relationship is completely to misunderstand the nature of these relationships. There is no such thing as meaningful consent within these sorts of relationships.

Meaningful consent, which is necessary for a just and emotionally satisfying sexual relationship, is absent in relationships that are shaped by a difference in power and role. Hence it is unethical for a counsellor or minister to pursue or agree to sexual activity within such a relationship. It is the sole responsibility of the minister or counsellor to ensure that boundaries are respected and sex does not enter this pastoral situation.

In pastoral ministry it is also incumbent upon the minister to understand the difference between 'consent' and 'acquiescence'. As the professional in the relationship it is the duty of the minister to maintain the boundaries, carefully to study the dynamics of transference and counter-transference and to have effective supervision when doing any one-to-one pastoral work, which involves any degree of 'counselling'.

Warning signs that a pastoral relationship is breaching boundaries

Most exploitative relationships develop slowly and insidiously. At first all seems well but over time the minister introduces elements into the relationship that cross boundaries. Somewhat like child sexual abuse the victim of exploitation is 'groomed' and may be unaware that what is happening is unethical and breaches professional guidelines for good pastoral care. Unfortunately the person may be so in need of nurturing or care that they misinterpret what is happening as care and affection. Many victims do want and need care and affection but this is not the same as 'consent' to a sexual relationship. Often when the relationship moves from 'care and affection' to sex the person seeking help is caught so deeply into the dependency that they are unable to extricate themselves or simply don't know how. Some people who have survived abuse, but have never learned what boundaries are all about or that sex does not always mean love, get incredibly confused when a minister sexualizes the pastoral relationship. They often feel flattered that a minister has 'chosen' them for this unique relationship and it becomes a confirmation in their minds that they are indeed worthy and valuable people. Such people have very low self-esteem and can only see 'value' in sexual terms following childhood sexual abuse.

There are indicators whan a relationship is crossing boundaries and moving towards a sexual one.[10] These warning signs describe the development of a relationship much as a love relationship might develop. In a pastoral setting where the minister is advising, counselling or spiritually directing a person such a development is unethical and exploitative. However, there are other variations, which use God or spiritual 'justifications' for the developing sexual engagement that is not in the 'romantic' vein above:

- believing that God has asked you to help the person sexually as a way of healing her or his abuse in childhood or other relationship problems;
- believing that in order to 'heal' a person sexually, intrusive sexual involvement is required to purify orifices which are contaminated by evil or the devil's 'entry' points;
- telling the person that sexual activity is holy and therefore not a sin or bad;
- telling the person that as an ordained person you can do them no harm as God is your guide.

Aftermath for the victim of clergy sexual exploitation

Violation of boundaries can be extremely damaging, with long-term consequences. An exploitative counsellor or minister disrupts the individual's sense of safety in the world. When this place shows itself to be unsafe, and there is a betrayal of trust, it can cause extreme distress that can lead to both physical and psychological illness. The additional damage, not so pertinent in secular clients, is that for the religious person the breach of trust will have a profound impact on his or her spiritual life and beliefs. Such damage may increase the fears and difficulties for the victim since they may fear God and eternal damnation. So the world becomes unsafe, and so too do death and the afterlife.

CHAPTER NINE

Causation: sexual abuse in the Church

On 5 November 1997, a panel of ecclesiastical judges called for the deposition of the Revd Clifford Williams. They accused him of adultery and leading a 'double life' within the Church in Wales and recommended that he be 'removed from the incumbency of his parish, expelled from the office of a cleric, and deposed from Holy Orders'.[1]

Increasingly, sexual abuse in the Church has become an issue of public concern. This is a phenomenon set in society and since the Church is set in society, this phenomenon is set within the Church. The secular conceptual frameworks that have evolved over the past 20 years to help us understand sexual abuse,[2] and the current theory-knitting work of Tony Ward and Richard Siegart,[3] all contribute to our understanding of the problem of sexual abuse in the Church.

This chapter will solely seek to understand sexual abuse in a Church context. It will look specifically at the prevalence of sexual abuse in the Church, consider the complex question of causation, review cycles of offending and conclude with recommendations for treatment and prevention drawn from an understanding of causation. Joe Sullivan suggests in *Notanews* that, 'It is impossible to intervene effectively in a process you do not understand'.[4] This chapter is about understanding. However, to understand is not to excuse an individual's responsibility for abusive behaviour. Greater understanding may help in the identification of ways to make the Church a safer environment.

There is evidence that there are higher levels of sexually abusive behaviour in the Church and by religious professionals than in other comparable caring professions. This was first suggested in research done by the editors of *Leadership*,[5] a professional magazine written for American Protestant clergy and separately, at about the same time, by the Revd Marie Fortune,[6] founder of the Center for the Study of Sexual and Domestic Violence in Seattle, Washington. Richard Sipe, writing from a Roman Catholic perspective in *Sex, Priests and Power*,[7] took much the same view.

Other reports have come in. For example, regarding the United Church of Canada,[8] research has suggested that clergy are 'exploiting their parishioners at twice the rate of secular therapists'. The most up to date research amongst Lutheran clergy in America[9] estimates that approximately 37 per cent have been involved in some form of sexual misconduct. Little research has yet been done in these islands to discover how common it is for ministers and clergy here to engage in inappropriate sexual behaviour. One study among Church of England clergy[10] showed that almost a quarter of its sample recognized that at some point in their ministry they had done something sexually inappropriate with someone other than their spouse. What that meant could range from inappropriate hugging or kissing through to full sexual abuse; respondents were not asked what they had done.

Additionally, the Group was particularly alarmed to hear from the director of the Wolvercote Clinic (a treatment centre for sexual offenders, currently closed), albeit as anecdotal evidence, that 25 per cent of the men in residence in his treatment centre for offences against children saw themselves as committed Christians. Fortune, in a paper delivered to the American Academy of Religion in 1992 and published in the *Journal of Feminist Studies*,[11] said of such abuse by clergy, other church leaders and religious professionals, that 'a secret long hidden has been disclosed'. This chapter asks what is going on to make this happen in the Church at twice the rate of secular helping professionals? Why is this going on at all? What would our knowledge of causation suggest about treatment and prevention?

Causation is usually attributed to one or more of the following six factors:

● human condition
● societal influence
● predatory persons
● psychological susceptibility
● risks in the role
● institutional failure.

The last three of these have been identified by the clergy of the Church of England as particularly relevant to understanding sexual abuse in the Church[12] and therefore more attention has been paid, in the rest of the chapter, to the implications of this part of the research data.

Human condition

This is the view that attributes sexual abuse in the Church to our fallen nature, the universal condition summed up in Romans 3.23 that 'All have sinned'. The Group, made up as it was of church members and church leaders, recognized throughout the work the reality and the universal nature of sin. This is considered at length in the chapter on theology. Our concern here is to understand the sociological and psychological functions and dysfunctions that are the substance of the sin and the outworking of our fallen human nature.

Societal factors

The sexual behaviour of church leaders and church members takes place within the sociological context of the mores and practices of the wider society. It cannot help but reflect in part, even in very exclusive churches, the prevailing attitudes of the times and of the cultural context. This is particularly true of churches made up mostly of 'second generation' rather than directly converted Christians.

In a postmodern society, sexual behaviour becomes a matter of choice. In our view there exists in our society a powerful and prevailing message that sexual activity is to be much sought after, a matter of individual choice and personal entitlement and necessary to personal fulfilment. Changing attitudes to sexuality, the economic emancipation of women and the women's movement, marriage and divorce, contraception, lesbian and gay equality, the Internet, the media and our capacity to travel to places of anonymity all have an impact on attitudes and sexual practices within and without the Church.

Sexual behaviour within the Church is not unaffected by such factors and takes place in the wider context of the values and characteristics of society in which the Church finds itself (see Chapter 2). However much we might wish for sexual behaviours to reflect our view of Christian values we recognize that even our view of Christian values is harnessed to our culture and the values of the wider society.

Predatory persons

In our research we have come across the idea that the responsibility for sexual abuse can sometimes be assigned to the person, usually the woman, who has been abused. Within Christian culture this has been to blame Adam's fall on Eve, and thus on the tempting and seductive nature of the other person. We recognize that in our society there has been a view that sexual indiscretion is in the allowable nature of men and therefore it is the woman's responsibility to refrain from sexual behaviour. This view has been persistently challenged by the women's movement and has little place in informed discussion, nevertheless we note it because, in places, this view remains. The effect of such a view is to make the person abused responsible for the abuse and to allow others, usually men, to abrogate responsibility. It cannot be overemphasized that this is a gender issue. Sexual abuse is something done, primarily by men, and primarily but not exclusively to women and children.

Psychological susceptibility

Clearly, church leaders are not exempt from the problems, difficulties and weaknesses that are part of the human condition. They bring to ministry the reality of their sexuality and the reality of the certainties and the uncertainties, the clarities and the confusions that exist for everyone in the outworking of the vicissitudes and victories of life. From our interviews and from a review of the relevant literature, there seem to be five particularly relevant factors within the personality and personal history of some church leaders and members pertinent to the issue of sexual abuse: sexual shame, sexual confusion, developmental uncertainties, narcissistic damage and addictive compulsive behaviours, including sexual addiction.

Narcissistic damage is probably the most crucial to understanding the relationship between sexual misconduct and religious behaviour and therefore this term needs to be defined and explained in greater detail. The term 'narcissistic damage' is used here to describe 'damage' to the construction and functioning of the self. It is the 'self experienced painfully', as 'less-than' and as 'in danger of fragmentation'. This experience is true for everyone, but some people adopt highly dysfunctional patterns of behaviour to regulate, conceal and relieve the pain of these distressed inner states. A detailed and substantiating analysis of the physiology of the self can be found in Daniel Stern's book *The Interpersonal World of the Infant*.[13]

Shame is a primary human emotion and the principal byproduct of narcissistic damage.[14] It can best be described as a profound sense of somehow being intrinsically flawed and, at the same time, a sense that, if others were to know, there would be fearful and painful consequences. Shame has the capacity to derail both cognition and coordination.[15] Sexual shame is a feeling that sexuality in general and one's own sexuality in particular is an intrinsically bad thing. High levels of sexual shame generate fear, a need to hide, discomfort with sexual information or behaviour, a need for secrecy, and an unconscious need to split off inner realities from outward appearances. Since the clergy and other church leaders are sexual beings as a condition of their humanity, they are caught in a trap: experiencing sexual desire and sexual need, and at the same time, experiencing shame and distress at the presence of these natural processes. The catch-22 of this predicament is that such shame can seek comfort in religion and at the same time can drive addictive compulsive behaviours. Among behavioural outcomes, there can emerge a whole range of problems, including a distinctive pattern of sexual abuse that is rooted in sexual addiction.[16]

In interviews with those who have abused others, it became clear that there was also a great deal of sexual confusion.[17] This manifested itself in a variety of ways: uncertainty about sexual functioning, sexual problems inside marriage, a loss of desire for sex, problems of courtship and relationship building, problems of accepting orientation and/or the implications of orientation for a responsible and ordered ministry. Although Fortune suggests that most sexual abuse in the Church is committed by adult heterosexual men against adult heterosexual women,[18] nevertheless in the in-depth interviews uncertainty and anxiety about sexual orientation featured. Such confusion and uncertainty adds to inner distress and may contribute to the propensity to abuse. The shame and the confusion are what lead to susceptibility and not issues of orientation. Sexual preference is not the problem; the problem is an outcome of institutional confusion, double standards and sexual shame. The high levels of homophobia prevailing in parts of the Church, especially in those who would see or present themselves as heterosexual, evidences high levels of covert or repressed homosexual interest in these same people[19] and, with that, more double standards and further shame, confusion and inner turmoil.

It is clear from an analysis of a series of interviews undertaken with clergy sexual offenders[20] that, at least among older Roman Catholic priests, many of these men have an arrested psychosexual development and have entered ministry with very little sexual experience, and little experience of or capacity for intimate relationships with either women or men. They bring, therefore, to adult church leadership a serious sexual and relationship immaturity. Sexual desire is not eliminated by a commitment to ministry. In one researcher's view[21] the expectations of celibacy and the nature of ministry, unfortunately, keep such men arrested, underdeveloped, secretive and susceptible to committing sexually abusive behaviours. It also seems that there is, quite commonly, a pattern of systematic or inter-generational abuse, in that those who abuse were, in fact, in some way also abused, though this is by no means universal, and our knowledge in this area is incomplete.

Sexual addiction is a concept that can help to explain some of the phenomena of sexual abuse that takes place both inside and outside the Church. Sexual addiction is defined as a pattern of sexual behaviour which is distinctive in that it cannot be reliably controlled and which brings with it harmful consequences.[22] It is characterized as a 'survival strategy' that is out of control, high risk, mood altering and inordinately time consuming.[23] There is often a desire to stop, or limit the behaviour, alongside a seeming inability to stop.[24] Addictions are embedded patterns of behaviour involving substances or processes that emerge to alleviate the feelings of narcissistic damage, especially feelings of shame, stress, loneliness and worthlessness. The idea of 'slavery' inherent in the notion of addiction is not without theological resonance, particularly in Paul, and later and more clearly apposite for our work, in Augustine. It is important to note that not all sexual addiction is abusive but rather that some abusive behaviours may be attached to patterns of sexual addiction.

All addictions, sexual addiction included, seem to emerge from narcissistic damage and narcissistic deprivation.[25] This is a 'family of origin' experience normally associated with impaired parenting, and with disturbance in the mother–child relationship in particular,[26] that brings with it a characteristic set of symptoms. These include, among others, loneliness, low self-esteem, boundary ambiguity, grandiosity, boredom, chronic envy, and the need for admiration.[27] Roles are taken to mask the inner sense of self and behaviours are adopted to soothe the inner sense of discomfort and neediness that accompanies narcissistic damage. The Church of England clergy who were consulted about causation[28] located sexual misconduct primarily in this symptomology: the neediness, loneliness and experienced stress of the clergy. Later in-depth interviews carried out with clergy sexual abusers seemed to confirm this same combination of factors in the causation of sexual abuse.

A number of writers have alluded to the relationship between narcissistic damage and the exercise of ministry.[29] Recent research at the University of Northern Colorado supports this view but also notes that high levels of narcissism characterize abusing and non-abusing clergy.[30] What seems to have gone largely unnoticed is the fact that religious behaviour and sexual behaviour can both be used to relieve the pain and distress of narcissistic wounding.[31] William James in Varieties of Religious of Experience,[32] using different language, strongly suggests such a process. More or less how this works can be explained by an exploration of the cycles of offending and/or the cycles of addiction considered later in this chapter.

It seems that some people with high levels of narcissistic damage utilize religious behaviour and other behaviours, including sexual behaviour, to mask and soothe the pain and shame of such damage. It is this combination, taken together or working alternatively, that may well help to explain the high levels of sexually abusive behaviour within the church. Such people, who are often high-performers and very capable in every way, then occupy roles that render them susceptible to sexually abusing others. They are then given no proper support or supervision and no awareness training or, for that matter, any other training in relationships, sexuality or human development. This in no way excuses the behaviour of individuals who abuse, but highlights action points for Churches in their endeavours to prevent future abuse.

Risks in the role

Sexual abuse in the Church has its origins and causation not only in the psychology of the individual but also in the power, nature and construction of ministry. The pastoral role is normally accorded high levels of moral authority but, also as it is practised, brings with it stress and boundary ambiguity.

The exercise of ministry is fraught with dual roles, boundary overlaps and indistinct demarcations. The same person can ask you for money, join you for dinner, sit with you in grief, take your children swimming, lead you in worship and join you for coffee when you are home alone. The boundaries are blurred between the ministerial office and personal friendship, between the house as personal space or as a tool of ministry, between the conversation at the pub as recreation or as evangelism.

The Oxford Diocese handbook *The Greatness of the Trust* emphasizes this point: 'The greatest dangers are the failure to recognize proper boundaries and a misunderstanding of the nature of pastoral relationships.'[33]

In a clergy focus group on this subject conducted in 1999 there was considerable and inconclusive discussion on the indistinguishable boundaries between professional and non-professional relationships.[34] The problems of blurred boundaries was emphasized as not a 'grey area' but with even greater complexity, 'varying shades of grey'. This is described ethically and professionally in the following:

> Clergy roles are inherently more complex and fraught with boundary strains... Health care professionals generally have much more circumscribed roles. In fact, some health care professions, such as psychology, consider such a complex role to be inherently unethical, because of dual relationships. In effect, some health care professions have determined that the extraordinary diversity of roles that clergy routinely play are simply impossible to manage appropriately, because of boundary strains.[35]

The maintenance and occupation of multiple roles in ministry has a long tradition and other options are probably not viable but, nevertheless, it is important to realize that this significantly contributes to the vulnerability of church leaders and clergy to breaches of trust.[36] This is sympathetically recognized in *Sex in the Parish*:

> The loneliness of the clergy, the close relationships they enter, the fact that they have intimate access to people's homes and bedrooms, the privacy and isolation of their own office settings – all these factors can be conducive to sexual desire and can contribute to the temptation to act on that desire.[37]

The possibility, and indeed probability, of sexual abuse in the Church is clearly connected, in part, to the boundary-blurring role ambiguity associated with traditional manifestations of Christian ministry.

In research with clergy of the Church of England almost all of the clergy interviewed or polled took the view that the vulnerability of the clergy to sexual misconduct is connected to the levels of stress associated with ministerial office. Andrew Irvine[38] writing on clergy stress emphasizes two important points: first the high level of stress, and secondly the source of stress in confusion, secrecy, role ambiguity and the conflict between the demands of individual authenticity and the requirements of public office. Additionally, church leaders experience isolation and often the absence of solicitous support. Where can these people honestly take problematic issues of sexuality? All the Roman Catholic clergy interviewed stressed this point without exception.[39] As the issues move into the arena of sexuality and the margins of misconduct, the stress is increased and the potential for misconduct increases in tandem.

It is important for us to understand that the aetiology of sexual abuse in the Church is associated not only with the individual psychology and susceptibility of the abuser to perpetrating acts of abuse but that there are serious contributing components inherent in the expectations of day-to-day ministry. None of this is written to excuse but rather to explain and clarify.

Institutional failure

In addition to the theological concepts and traditions of belief (examined in chapter 11) that provide a conducive context for sexual abuse there are a number of ecclesiological factors that seem to contribute directly to the aetiology of sexual abuse in the Church.

In a letter to the Editor of the *Guardian* about the Clifford Williams affair, Margaret Kennedy of the Minister and Clergy Sexual Abuse

Survivors Group called for the Church to have 'policies to challenge similar and abusive predatory behaviour'.[40] In research done with Church of England clergy on this subject, Birchard[41] took the view that factors of institutional failure and negligence were seriously responsible for the problem of sexual abuse in the Church. These factors included the following:

- absence of awareness training
- absence of pastoral care, supervision, accountability of the ministers
- absence of codes of professional ethics
- absence of an adequate theology of sexuality
- sexism endemic in the Church
- a culture of silence and secrecy.

In research done with Roman Catholic offenders against children[42] the offenders themselves were unanimous in their view that the absence of awareness training and the absence of teaching on issues of human development contribute to the problems of sexual misconduct in the Church. Of the Church of England clergy who responded to a survey on causation, 91 per cent attributed significant causation to the absence of awareness training in theological colleges, as well as in other places of continuing ministerial education. Similarly, in other parts of this same research, causation was tied, over and over again, to the absence of awareness training, the absence of pastoral care and the absence of supervision.

Penny Jamieson writing from an Anglican perspective in *Living on the Edge*[43] identifies the culture of secrecy and the 'circle of silence' as especially conducive to sexual abuse in the Church. Richard Sipe[44] makes exactly the same point in his book on sexual abuse in the Roman Catholic Church. Other writers confirm this view[45] which is consistent with the findings of the *Report on Sexual Harassment and Abuse* in the Methodist Church.[46]

We have observed a tendency for the hierarchies of both the Roman Catholic Church and the Church of England to deflect attention from this institutional failure by focusing responsibility on the individual members of the pastorate. This loses track of the fact that such people were chosen by the institution, formed and trained by the institution, and commissioned to minister in a system of oversight and care designed and supported by the institution. We would be concerned if Church hierarchies and other bodies of leadership tried to scapegoat the ministers in an attempt to deflect blame away from the shortcomings of the senior leadership and the governing bodies of the Church.

Typology and cycles of sexual abuse

It will help us to understand sexual abuse in the Church if we look at a typology of offending and at several of the models that have been developed by theoreticians and clinicians to describe the phenomenology that lies behind abuse, sexual addiction and offending.

The Centre for the Prevention of Sexual and Domestic Violence, in its literature, roughly divided sexual offenders into two types: the 'wanderer' and the 'predator'.[47] These are self-explanatory categories. 'Predator' would signify an exploitative pattern of sexual behaviour involving differentials of power that is pathological, cyclical, recurrent and enduring. The 'wanderer' is characterized as someone who wanders into sexual misconduct almost by accident, more out of naïvety and vulnerability than out of any deep-seated repetitive pathology. In an interview in *Leadership* magazine, Bud Palmer says: 'for most of us in local church ministry, sexual temptation doesn't come painted in the lurid tones of a vamp. It comes in the quiet, gentle relationships a pastor has with people he truly loves.'[48]

This same view was echoed in a focus group of Church of England clergy.[49] One of the participants talked about 'almost slipping unawares into a relationship with the person with whom one is working'.

Many professional codes of conduct restrict or preclude sexual and romantic relationships with clients or others for whom one is professionally responsible. For example the Code of Conduct and Practice of the British Association for Sexual and Relationship Therapy never allows a sexual or marital relationship between a therapist and client under any circumstances or at any time in the future. In church life, by contrast, it is still often customary to expect an unmarried curate to court the churchwarden's daughter or a teacher in a church school or to find a wife from the parish. One of the clergy focus groups took the view that it was entirely proper for a clergyperson to court a member of the congregation.[50] This perspective was noted and promoted by Lebacqz and Barton:

> We have ample evidence from our own circle of friends and acquaintances to suggest that it can and does happen that pastor and parishioner can meet as equals, become romantically and sexually involved, and enter solid and committed relationships.[51]

At the time of writing, Karen Lebacqz was Professor of Christian Ethics at Berkeley and Ronald Barton the Associate Conference Minister for the United Church of Christ in San Francisco. Clearly this issue of clergy courtship raises important ethical questions and signals the need for practical policies of care and supervision. For example, in the Episcopal Church in the Diocese of New York a priest is required to make a private but official declaration of an intention to courtship to an appropriate diocesan authority if the person is a member of his or her congregation. This applies to same-gender as well as cross-gender relationships. The point of this process is to bring the relationship to responsible knowledge. Other Churches could devise similar approaches adapted to their own ecclesial structure. Abuse operates in circumstances of secrecy and silence. If we accept that it is ethically correct for a church leader to be in a developing romantic and sexual relationship with a member of the church, which is the nature of courtship, then there needs to be some way of protecting both parties and excepting this behaviour from designation as sexual abuse. This is especially true since not all courtships have a happy, or mutually desired, outcome.

There are a number of 'models of understanding' and cycles of behaviour that we can call upon to help further our understanding of sexual abuse. Four of these are evaluated, criticized and knit together in new work by Tony Ward, Professor of Forensic Psychology, University of Melbourne, in his book (co-edited with S. Hudson) *Theory and Sexual Offending*.[52] His own 'good lives' model of offender treatment has much to commend it to the Church as it tailors offender treatment to the needs of the individual and it moves offender treatment beyond containment to problem resolution and the development of a fulfilling lifestyle.

Because of limited space only two 'cycles of sexual behaviour' will be described in this paper, although four are illustrated. These are cited to aid an understanding of the process that lies behind abusive sexual behaviour: the first is the 'cycle of offending' developed by Wolf and described and developed further by Joe Sullivan (see fig. 2 on p. 94);[53] the second is that outlined by David Finkelhor and also modified by Joe Sullivan[54] and discussed in Tony Ward's new book (see fig. 3 on p. 95); the third the cycle of addiction outlined by Patrick Carnes (see fig. 4 on p. 96); the fourth is the shame-bound cycle of Fossum and Mason (see fig. 5 on p. 97).

Wolf's work is at the centre of most cognitive-behavioural sex offender treatment programmes.[55] It is self-explanatory and relatively simple to understand; therefore it is shown here in diagram form without further comment.

Figure 2. S. Wolf, 'The cycle of offending' (1984)

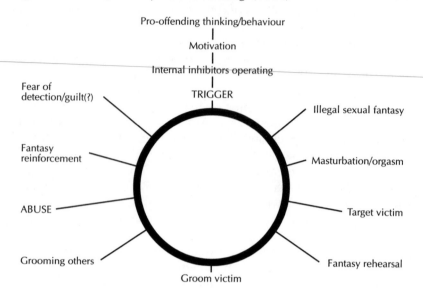

Finkelhor's work, which explores motivational causation, has also been of vital importance in the development of treatment of those who have offended and significantly underpins much rehabilitation work (fig. 3).

Carnes' work has been strategic in the development of our understanding sexual addiction and sexual compulsivity (fig. 4). It is important to remember that sexual abuse may involve adults or children, and that not all sexual addiction is abuse and that not all abuse is addiction.

Four-preconditions model of sexual abuse

Figure 3. D. Finkelhor, 'A clinical application' (1986) and adapted by Joe Sullivan

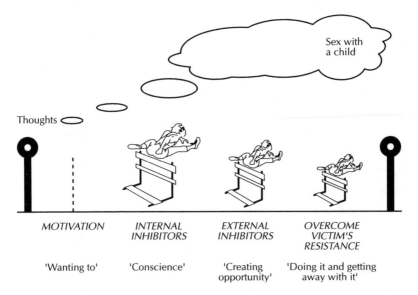

MOTIVATION	INTERNAL INHIBITORS	EXTERNAL INHIBITORS	OVERCOME VICTIM'S RESISTANCE
'Wanting to'	'Conscience'	'Creating opportunity'	'Doing it and getting away with it'

This model was developed by David Finkelhor to address previous shortcomings in theory development and to provide a more comprehensive framework to explain child sexual abuse. He suggests[56] that all factors relating to child sexual abuse can be grouped as contributing to one of four preconditions. All four need to be met before abuse occurs:

1. A potential offender needed to have some motivation to abuse a child sexually.
2. The potential offender had to overcome internal inhibitions against acting on that motivation.
3. The potential offender had to overcome external impediments to committing sexual abuse.
4. The potential offender or some other factor had to undermine or overcome a child's possible resistance to sexual abuse.

Motivation might include such things as arrested emotional development, re-enactment, narcissistic identification, and inappropriate patterns of arousal. Internal disinhibitors could include alcohol use, impulse disorders or the failure of incest inhibition mechanisms in family dynamics. He lists as examples of external disinhibitors: an absent mother, social isolation, lack of supervision, unusual opportunities to be alone with the child. Factors cited in overcoming the child's resistance include coercion, unusual trust between the child and the offender, insecurity and deprivation. In summarizing this model Finkelhor writes:

> Sexual abuse is a problem with causes and explanations. Many of these we do not fully understand. The four pre-conditions model is open-ended; new findings and new ideas can be added to it. By having given some structure to what is already known, this model enables us to use that knowledge.[57]

These four preconditions interact with the six attributed causes, discussed earlier in this chapter, and which provide the 'filler' for the four preconditions.

The addictive system

Figure 4. P. Carnes, 'The addictive system' (*Out of the Shadows*, 1983)

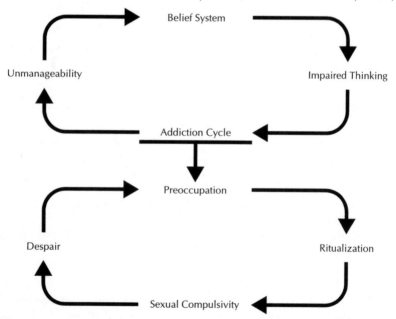

Patrick Carnes in *Out of the Shadows*[58] outlines a cycle of addiction that operates in alternating rhythms of control and release. It is set in a faulty belief system that supports impaired thinking and operates with a four-phase cycle of preoccupation, ritualization, sexual compulsivity and despair. The lives of addicts, he says, become immersed in this control–release cycle. Carnes later writes in *Don't Call It Love:* 'when in the process of sexual acting out there is a total absorption in the behaviour, a numbing of all judgements and expectations'.[59] The cycle is driven by shame and shame is the principal byproduct of narcissistic damage. Carnes writes again as follows:

> The addict's intense emotional pain is transformed into pleasure during the preoccupation and ritualization stages, becoming euphoria during the fleeting moments of sexual release. However, following the climax experience, the addict plummets into shame and despair more deeply with each repetition of the cycle. Isolation also increases.[60]

Once the behaviour is completed, or that part of the cycle exhausted, then there is a period of control, characterized by avoidance and doing good, until a sense of need or entitlement sets off the next stage of the cycle. These cycles can operate at frequent and infrequent intervals and they can operate systemically in conjunction with family members or chosen others.[61]

Figure 5. M. Fossum and M. Mason, 'The shame-bound cycle' (*Facing Shame,* 1986)

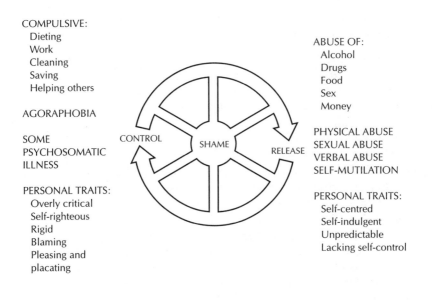

COMPULSIVE:
  Dieting
  Work
  Cleaning
  Saving
  Helping others

AGORAPHOBIA

SOME
PSYCHOSOMATIC
ILLNESS

PERSONAL TRAITS:
  Overly critical
  Self-righteous
  Rigid
  Blaming
  Pleasing and
  placating

CONTROL   SHAME   RELEASE

ABUSE OF:
  Alcohol
  Drugs
  Food
  Sex
  Money

PHYSICAL ABUSE
SEXUAL ABUSE
VERBAL ABUSE
SELF-MUTILATION

PERSONAL TRAITS:
  Self-centred
  Self-indulgent
  Unpredictable
  Lacking self-control

This conceptual model seems especially important for understanding sexual abuse in the Church because it helps explain the juxtaposition of the two apparently incompatible behaviours: sexual abuse and religious service. It is likely that in many of the cases of abuse in the Church, sexual and religious behaviours alternate in a repeating cycle of control and release. This is the same structure as the binge–purge cycle characteristic of eating disorders. From the interviews done with clergy offenders[62] it is clear that the sexual abuse committed by these men followed this pattern. Sexual episodes, over which there is often denial, justification, profound shame and great fear, and ultimately despair, are followed by zealous commitments to hard work, abstinence, devotion, service and righteousness. Eventually a sense of need or entitlement emerges, internal and external inhibitors are overcome and the cycle begins again.

About such cycles of abuse and circles of addiction, perhaps there is much to learn from Augustine:

> The enemy had my power of willing in his clutches, and from it had forged a chain to bind me. The truth is that disordered lust springs from a perverted will; when lust is pandered to, a habit is formed; when the habit is not checked, it hardens into a compulsion. These were interlinking rings forming what I have described as a chain, and my harsh servitude used it to keep me under duress.[63]

His knowledge of the nature of addiction and offending, his imagery of the chains of habituation, addiction and slavery, and his experience of its resolution in the paradox of powerlessness, suggests that we should read the *Confessions* again, with fresh eyes.

Review and summary

Current thinking would accept that sexual abuse in the Church is not just about sex. When committed by a church leader against a staff member or a church member, it is an abuse of power and violates the duty of care and conditions of trust implicit in the pastoral relationship. Marie Fortune[64] describes this, not just as a misuse of power, but also as a violation of role, an exploitation of the vulnerable, and as an act that, because of the difference in role, precludes meaningful consent.

Until recently there has been little suggestion in the literature, or in our knowledge of current practice, that it is possible to test for a 'potential to abuse' and thus to create a screening system for the Church. However, the NSPCC has developed a process of value-based interviews for prospective employees to identify problems with boundaries, among other things. The NSPCC is also developing a selection tool to attempt to screen out people with a propensity to abuse. These developments are still at an early stage but may inform churches as they consider the implications of this report for the recruitment, selection, training and supervision of those in positions of pastoral responsibility.

The three major factors that account for sexual misconduct in the Church seem to be the personal problems of the church leader, especially problems that somehow seek both a religious and a sexual solution, aspects of ministerial service that create vulnerability to sexual misconduct, and the ignorant and inattentive character of the institution. Any of these alone might lead a man or woman to such behaviour, but all taken together they have created the multitude of pastoral problems and reactive media explosions we see happening all around us.

The high levels of sexual abuse in the Church can be explained by this combination: powerful but susceptible people with sexual and personal problems, in stressful jobs without boundaries, working with other people often vulnerable and needy and without boundaries, in an organization without training or supervision, in an ecclesiastical culture dominated by sexual shame and endemic secrecy.

CHAPTER TEN

Responding to those who abuse

This chapter offers a brief review of some of the issues involved in responding to those who abuse. Several denominations have produced reports and developed procedures within the past few years regarding the response which the Churches should make to people who have committed sexual offences. This Report does not go over the same ground in detail but affirms the good work that has already been done and encourages those Churches still to tackle these issues to consider what has been done by others.

These issues are far from simple. All the evidence makes it quite clear that there are many more people who have abused than are identified, let alone prosecuted and convicted. Often, churches deal not with certainties but with suspicions and informal comments about people being uncomfortable with other people's behaviour.

When an allegation is actually made, churches increasingly have internal procedures that come into play and external agencies are involved at an early stage. If the allegation is not proceeded with, churches have to decide what to do in the light of that. Where an allegation against a person becomes a criminal charge and the person is acquitted, that is rarely the end of the story. The person may proclaim their 'innocence'. This may well be the case. At the same time, a 'not guilty' verdict is not the same as 'innocent'. The burden of proof ('beyond all reasonable doubt') in criminal cases makes a conviction by no means a foregone conclusion. Sometimes, after a person has been acquitted, churches are approached by statutory agencies and given information that would make it very unwise to allow the person against whom the allegations were made to be in direct contact with children and young people.

When a person is given an official caution or conviction the law now demands that such a person may not work with children and young people in future. Some churches have gone further and not only prevent them working with children and young people but do not allow such offenders to hold other offices in the church either. However, this has been a controversial step. Some Christian people believe it flies in the face of Christian teaching about forgiveness. When forgiveness is seen in terms of wiping the slate clean, people may find it hard to accept that offenders are told they may never hold office in the church again. Other Christians point to the link between forgiveness and repentance, and argue that a forgiven offender must accept the need not to enter into behaviours that in the past led to offending. The theological issues relating to forgiveness are dealt with more fully in Chapter 11.

A starting point for a church congregation is likely to be a desire to welcome everybody and anybody into a congregation. All are sinners. All need forgiveness. All need healing. People who have committed sexual offences are no different from anyone else in these respects. What is more, having served a prison sentence and perhaps coming into a new community while trying to build a new life, a sex offender will benefit from the support of a caring community. The Methodist report, *The Church and Sex Offenders,*[1] suggests an offender needs to receive from the church community, 'acceptance, love, a place to worship and join in fellowship, comrades for the journey, and people who accept him as he is and commit themselves to supporting him in his attempt to live a new life as a recovering sex offender.' As a member of the church community such a person will naturally want not just to receive from the community but to give back. At this point, if the church puts limits on ways in which he or she may do this, the person may feel rejected and not fully accepted as a member of the community. Yet the church clearly has to consider the needs not only of the offender but of people who have been victims/survivors of abuse and those who might become victims.

Shortly after the Methodist Conference adopted its report in 2000, the *News of the World* ran its 'Name and shame' campaign, in which it printed photographs and details of convicted sex offenders now living in the community. A great deal of media attention and public debate was focused on the issue and it became clear how difficult it is for released offenders to find a place within the community. Local communities campaign against the provision of accommodation or treatment centres for offenders within their area. Churches may have a role to play in making the community safer both from and for sex offenders.

As mentioned in the opening paragraph to this chapter, several Churches have done work on how to respond to those who abuse. For example in 1999 the Board of Social Responsibility of the Church of England published *Meeting the Challenge: How Churches Should Respond to Sex Offenders.*[2] The British Methodist Conference adopted their report on *The Church and Sex Offenders*[3] in 2000. In September 2001, the Catholic Bishops' Conference of England and Wales published *A Programme for Action: The Final Report of the Independent Review on Child Protection in the Catholic Church in England and Wales*[4] (the Nolan Report). As a result of the report's recommendations, a National Child Protection Unit has been set up and one of its tasks is 'to prepare and issue guidance on arrangements to enable the safe participation of former child abusers in the life of the Church'.

In the Introduction to *Meeting the Challenge*,[5] The Rt Revd Richard Harries wrote, 'the instinct of Christian compassion is to be generous, but this proper spirit needs to be tempered by the risk sex offenders pose and the manipulative strategies they use'. The document lists some of the methods sex offenders often use to try and perpetrate their offences – methods that must make churches wary:

- They often minimize the extent of their offending or may deny it entirely.
- They like people to believe they are 'nice guys' and may try to impress others with the depth of their Christian commitment.
- Sex offenders use a process of 'grooming' to 'target' their victims (and may well 'groom' not only the individual potential victim, but their family and the church community).
- Sex offenders often move around from job to job and place to place, so that their activities are not easily monitored.
- Sex offenders have distorted belief systems that are very well established. Treatment programmes may help control their activities, but find it harder to change their beliefs.
- Sex offenders (especially those who have served a prison sentence) often experience a conversion experience and embrace the Christian faith wholeheartedly. This is often a way of deflecting people from the reality of their offending as well as a way of covering up the grooming process they are operating. It can also be a way of avoiding responsibility for their offences.
- Sex offenders come from all backgrounds, classes and professions.
- Sex offenders are known for their resistance to change. People who work with them know that effecting change is part of a long-term process.

The good practice recommended by *Meeting the Challenge* includes the following:

- liaising with diocesan and parish child protection officers (who are likely to have links with external agencies);
- maybe set up a small group to befriend and keep a careful watch on the person;
- if you are concerned about someone's inappropriate behaviour, tell someone and make sure that person is not left alone with children and young people;
- explore what confidentiality means in this situation (so that it does not preclude sharing essential information);

- offer support to families of sex offenders, who are 'often forgotten victims'.

Appendix iii of *Meeting the Challenge* provides the following information sheet on how to plan the integration of known offenders.

> Where a known offender joins a church it will be important to extend love and friendship to the individual, but at the same time the leadership will need to ensure that a frank discussion takes place with the person concerned and efforts are made to sustain open communications.

> It will be necessary to establish clear boundaries for both the protection of the young people and to lessen the possibility of the adult being wrongly accused of abuse. The following points should be addressed:

- Church leaders should ensure they maintain close links with a probation officer (if any)
- be open with the offender
- prepare a contract which includes:-
  - attending designated meetings only
  - sitting apart from children
  - staying away from areas of the building where children meet
  - attending a house group where there are no children
  - declining hospitality where there are children
  - never being alone with children
  - never working with children
- get the offender to sign the contract
- enforce the contract – do not allow them to manipulate you
- consider whether to tell the church
- ensure key leaders know the situation (if you don't tell the church)
- provide close support and pastoral care
- ban the offender from church if the contract is broken and tell other churches or probation officer.

The Methodist report introduced a similar process, adding the encouragement that where possible liaison would take place between a prison chaplain and the receiving church before an offender is released. Methodist procedures require that a small group should always be set up and one of the first tasks for the group is to carry out a risk assessment (preferably involving those with statutory responsibility for the offender) of the risks present in the particular church building and its programme of events along with the risks presented by the particular offender's past behaviour. This risk assessment would be the basis for deciding the terms of the 'contract' to be made with the offender. It may be that not all churches or congregations can provide the personnel to set up a small group or the procedures for supporting and monitoring an offender. In this case it may be necessary to point the offender in the direction of a different church where the proper provision can be made. While it is still 'early days', experience and expertise in dealing with such arrangements is now developing within the denominations and with the help of external agencies such as the Churches' Child Protection Advisory Service (CCPAS). The Anglican Diocese of Southwell, for example, has taken up these ideas very carefully and their most recent version of the Diocesan Code of Practice to protect children and young people contains a chapter on 'Perpetrators of Child Sexual Abuse' with advice about pastoral care combined with an agreement by the perpetrator (see p. 156). They have also tried to work ecumenically and have produced a document entitled *Better Together – Safeguarding Children: An Ecumenical Approach in Nottingham and Nottinghamshire.*

While the churches have increasingly shown their willingness and ability to work with other statutory and voluntary agencies, experience suggests they are not always consulted at a national or local level, even where they may have a significant contribution to make. This seems strange in a context where the Government is openly advocating a multi-agency approach involving relevant statutory and voluntary bodies.

The Nolan Report set up national standards in child protection to be adopted at diocesan and parish level. It also outlined procedures for whistle blowing and for the making and investigating of allegations. Particular attention is paid to situations in which the allegations are made against priests and deacons (including recommendations relating to the support to be offered to such a person both while the allegation is investigated and after a decision is made). It is important to note that in some other churches it is not priests or ministers but other people who have most frequently been prosecuted for abuse (children's workers or their spouses, caretakers, organists, etc.) The Nolan Report discusses whether laicization should be the outcome for priests and deacons cautioned or convicted for child abuse offences, and argues that it would 'not be a proportionate response in every case' (but would be the normal outcome where a person was sentenced to prison for 12 months or more). However, the report recommends that, 'as a general rule, clergy and lay workers who have been cautioned or convicted of an offence against children should not be allowed to hold any position that could possibly put children at risk again'.

Some other Churches have taken a different line and automatically dismiss a minister convicted of such offences. On the issue of offenders present in the congregation, the Nolan Report noted the procedure already established in some other Churches (e.g. the Church of England and Methodist Church procedures outlined above) and recommended a similar procedure for the Catholic Church.

Legislation

The British and Irish Governments have both passed a considerable amount of legislation relating to sexual offenders over the past decade or so.

For example, in England and Wales, under the Criminal Justice Act 1991, as subsequently amended, sex offenders who have served over twelve months in prison are supervised by the probation service for a statutory period following release. During this period the person has to report regularly to his or her probation officer, disclose any change of address and report any movement around the country. Before their release, a pre-discharge assessment is undertaken on such offenders, to consider what risk they pose and how that risk will be managed after the offender's release. Often, one of the terms of a licence will be that the offender must attend a groupwork programme similar to the sex offender treatment programmes run in a number of prisons. (The Group believes that even after attending such programmes it is probably better to think of an offender as 'recovering' rather than 'recovered'.)

Section 58 of the Crime and Disorder Act 1998 enables a judge to order that a sex offender is subject to extended licence of up to ten years on release. Police, probation and social services (sometimes along with other agencies) form area risk management conferences, whose task is to manage the risk posed by offenders living in their area.

The Act also allows a chief officer of police to apply to the magistrates' court for a sex offender to be put on a sex offender order. Such an order will be for five or more years and will place such prohibitions on the offender as are deemed necessary in order to protect the public from serious harm from the person.

The Sex Offenders Act 1997 introduced the registration of sex offenders released from 1 September 1997, but was not retrospective. A person convicted of or cautioned for particular sexual offences has to notify the local police of their name and home address and any subsequent changes in either. The requirements apply for a minimum period of five years, but for seven years where the person has been sentenced to less than six months' imprisonment, ten years where sentenced to between six and thirty months and indefinitely where the person is sentenced to thirty months' imprisonment or more.

The Police Act 1997 set up the Criminal Records Bureau (see Chapter 4). The Criminal Records Bureau now makes it easier for churches in the UK to check the criminal record of anyone seeking to work with children and young people. Already, most churches were asking applicants to sign a declaration saying they had no such convictions. But, of course, many perpetrators do not have convictions so the need for churches to be vigilant and develop good practice cannot be relaxed.

The Protection of Children Act 1999 provides for a list to be kept of those considered unsuitable for work with children. It is an offence for a person with a conviction for a sexual offence to apply for a job involving children.

The Criminal Justice and Court Services Act 2000, sections 67 and 68, creates a duty for police and probation services to make joint arrangements for the assessment and management of the risks posed by sexual, violent and other offenders to the public. Each year police and probation have to produce a joint annual report on arrangements made in the previous year.

Britain's laws on sex offences are currently under review and a government white paper is to be published in autumn 2002. It is likely that the concept of incest will be extended to cover step-parents. A new crime of 'adult sexual activity with a child' is likely to replace a number of current offences relating to different age limits and carrying different penalties.

In the Republic of Ireland, in 1999 the Protection of Persons Reporting Child Abuse Act and the Child Trafficking and Pornography Act came into force. The Sex Offenders Act 2001 created a sex offenders register, made it an offence for an offender not to declare the conviction, and allowed orders to be made for supervision of those discharged from prison.

In addition to legislation directly relating to sexual offending and child protection, there has been other legislation with indirect influence. In particular, data protection and human rights legislation affect the treatment of those against whom allegations are made and limit ways in which information that is not in the public domain is shared. The Freedom of Information Act in the Republic of Ireland has raised concerns about the need to ensure reports to the authorities are marked 'privileged'. The full effects of this legislation will not become clear until case law develops. It is also true that the Human Rights Act, in so far as children also have human rights, can be a powerful tool to protect them.

The role of churches

To offer pastoral support to both people who have experienced abuse and people who have abused is not easy. The presence of someone with a known history of sexual offending within a congregation will make it difficult if not impossible for people who have experienced abuse to feel safe. Some congregations will find it impossible – and it may be necessary to encourage someone who has abused to move to a church where the appropriate arrangements can be made. At the same time, evidence suggests that providing appropriate support to offenders helps prevent and minimize their risk of further offending.

There may be some church communities or individuals who feel they can offer a particular ministry of supporting those who have committed sexual offences as they seek to establish a new life back in the community. One model currently being piloted in partnership between probation, police and prison services along with Quaker Peace and Social Witness is that of Circles of Support and Accountability. The concept is relatively simple. A small number of volunteers (between 4 and 6) is recruited from the local community in which a high-risk sex offender is living. The Circle provides a support network for the offender, who is known as the 'core member', while also holding the person accountable for their actions. It will be important to see the results from these Home Office funded pilots.

When churches have developed procedures for the involvement of offenders in the life of the church, it is important to promote wide awareness of precisely what would happen (in terms of support group, risk assessment, contract, monitoring, etc.) if an offender joined the congregation. This information is particularly important for people who have been abused as they are likely to ask (and certainly need to know) how they will be kept safe. It needs to be clear whom they can go and talk to if they feel frightened, worried or hurt.

It is particularly important that churches consider the impact of what they do with and for offenders on those who have experienced abuse. *Time for Action* has been written because too often the Churches (and wider society) have failed to listen to their stories and see how things appear from their perspective. Churches owe those who have experienced abuse a duty of special care and support.

CHAPTER ELEVEN

'Christ is like a single body': some theological reflection

A religious community which does not hunger and thirst for justice to be done bears false witness.

Prophetic voices are those that read the signs of the times in the light of the justice and love of God, and speak out against all that distorts or diminishes the image of God in human beings. In doing so, they may come into conflict with the status quo, with powerful interests that have an investment in the way things are. They may struggle with questions of resisting and confronting established power. The Old Testament scholar Walter Brueggemann, reflecting on Israel as a community of intentional resistance to the oppressive power of Egypt, identifies what he calls 'liturgical resistance', the imagination of a free space outside the hegemony of the oppressor. Through the regular re-enactment of the Exodus story, using poetry, sacrament, sign and drama, it provides a script for an alternative practice, which incorporates:

● the public voicing of pain
● a critique that ridicules established power
● the song and dance of the women as a gesture of defiance.[1]

It seems that what we are seeing and hearing now is a kind of modern version of that resistance, as women especially, but those who have survived abuse generally, break through barriers of culture, nationality, religion, politics and status with a public voicing of their pain that says: we will no longer keep silent about this, it is no longer acceptable to hide the wounds, to cover up for those who have perpetrated abuse, to maintain the front of respectability. This presents huge challenges to the Church, in its spirituality, liturgy and theology.

Remembering the body

Gather us in, the lost and the lonely, the broken and breaking, the tired and the aching, Who long for the nourishment found at your feast.[2]

So what does it mean to be a person in the Christian community who has survived sexual abuse? To begin with, it means to remember.

Our sense memories – smell, taste, touch, sight, sound – are extremely powerful. Words collect emotional and physical responses and hold them in the body. It is the body which remembers first; memory is what brings to mind what is already in the body. We feel the sense memory in the body – and then we feel the emotional response that collected it in the first place: the curiosity, the delight, the wonder – or the fear, the pain, the anger. Human memory may be immediate, short-term or long-term, and what we choose to store in our long-term memory is closely linked to our emotions. We recreate in memory the context for the feeling. Our past reshapes our present.

Each community also has its mementoes and shared ceremonies which serve as reminders, which call to mind significant and formative events in its life. By these they are constituted, they know themselves and are known by others. It is a recollection. To re-member the body, whether it is the body personal or the body politic is to have a story, a history. And therefore, it is really to have a self: 'Memory is the self, because it is my presence to myself, the way in which I constitute myself and understand myself as a subject with a continuous history of experience.'[3] The freer and fuller our ability to remember, the freer and fuller our selves are able to be in the present. This, of course, is one of the foundation stones of therapeutic processes such as counselling. But it is not just in therapy that this is true.

It is recognized, for example, that the structured sharing of memories of elderly people is beneficial not just for its social opportunities but in its effects on physical and mental health. It is not enough just to have the memories; it is also important to share them. Telling our stories in the context of a shared understanding of their meaning and significance validates and confirms us in our identity. It gives us access to a fuller and freer self. This too is a gathering together, a recollection of all the members in a unity of purpose.

> We come to share our stories
> We come to break the bread
> We come to know our rising from the dead.[4]

Christian faith is premised on memory, on the recalling to mind of what we already know in the body. The great drama of liturgy is, in a sense, reminiscence. In worship, we become what the past is doing now.

And the whole Christian Church, which is constituted on memory, gives thanks as it gathers.

> We thank you for the memories
> that fill our minds today;
> for the Church that once received us
> and kept us in your way;
> for the ones that introduced us
> to Jesus Christ our Lord;
> for the saints who have known and loved us,
> our God, you are adored.[5]

When we gather to worship, the first thing we do is a naming. We are people who gather together under and in the name of Christ. We give ourselves the Christian name.

Or rather, we might say, it is the name that has been given to us. We are present in worship because, in an extraordinary variety of ways, *we have heard our name spoken*. And in that instant, we have recognized ourselves. That flash of recognition, of being known and named, becomes a place of gospel that we go back to again and again. And it is not just a personal identity we receive. It becomes our *common story*. We are people who have been named, and we gather with others who have shared that experience. So we recognize not only ourselves but each other.

You will be called by a new name . . .

> I will show love to those who were called 'Unloved' and to those who were called 'Not-My-People' I will say, 'You are my people' and they will answer 'You are our God.' (Isaiah 62.2; Hosea 2.23)

The words of the Hebrew prophets express poetically a reality which we cannot always explain prosaically; that somehow we show up grasping towards a different identity as those gathered together in Christ's name. We are named personally and we are named into a community.

Speaking of baptism, our ceremony of naming, Rowan Williams has written:

> the sacramental action itself traces a transition from one sort of reality to another; first it describes a pre-sacramental state, a secular or profane condition now imagined, for ritual purposes, in the light of and in the terms of the

transformation that is to be enacted; it tells us that where we habitually are is not, after all, a neutral place but a place of loss or need. It then requires us to set aside this damaged or needy condition, this flawed identity, so that in dispossessing ourselves of it we are able to become possessed of a different identity, given in the rite, not constructed by negotiation and co-operation like other kinds of social identity. The rite requires us not to belong any more to the categories we thought we belonged in, so that a distinctive kind of new belonging can be realized.[6]

The drama of worship, then, begins with a greeting given in Christ's name, and an invitation: to remember the personal and corporate event of *our* naming, to remember its meaning and significance for our lives, and to proclaim and reclaim it once more as a lived experience with consequences not just in the past but for the present and the future. But to minister the word made flesh when people gather together in Christ's name, we have to remember the body!

The memory of abuse: the public voicing of pain

> **Shame, or not shame**
> *I never know.*
> *I know that all the messages of flesh*
> *and blood scream at me, 'Shame, you should feel shame,*
> *you are not clean, you do not measure up*
> *to what the standard is.'*[7]

For many, perhaps most people, when we come to church, it is with a positive experience of the God who meets us, and we remember ourselves as having been named with love and acceptance.

But what if memory is not the recollection of enlarging, life-enhancing experience? What if it does not validate our identity but undermines and threatens it? What if the well from which we drink is poisoned? What of those whose memories may be hateful or hurtful?

One of the most unpleasant realities for survivors, in the midst of many unpleasant realities, is the recasting of memory as a malevolent force. The memories of those who have experienced sexual abuse, particularly child sexual abuse, may be so terrible that they undermine a person's integrity and sense of themselves to a profound degree. And if one cannot trust *these* memories are any of one's memories in fact trustworthy? Is one's whole self as what the past is doing now fatally flawed because the past is so unreliable?

This undermining is all too often reinforced by the reactions of people to whom the story of the one who has survived the abuse is told or becomes known. The story may simply be too appalling, too shocking, for others to be able to apprehend it. They cannot believe such things can happen. They do not *want* to believe such things can happen. If the one who has perpetrated the abuse is someone known to the church community, it is far worse. That person may well be known to them as an upstanding member of the church, a pillar of the community, someone who does good works and who they have conceived of as trustworthy. They may be a parish councillor, an elder, a choirmaster or youth leader. They may be the minister, priest or pastor. The congregation are familiar with the offender's public persona, which appears, and may well actually be, admirable. To recognize that in private, behind closed doors, someone may act in an altogether different way, is hard; though all of us, to some degree, wear a public face which we relax or lay aside in private where it is safe to do so, we hope that there is a reasonable degree of consistency between public and private. But where the disjunction is as acute as it is in the case of sexual abuse, it is terribly hard to reconcile the two faces. It makes us question our own judgement. We too begin to doubt our memories. A past which has seemed solid is subjected to radical revisioning. What we thought were good memories were apparently not. What had seemed shared recollection becomes shared alienation.

This deeply unsettling process affects all communities where someone with authority is discovered to have been abusing, whether it is a school, a business, a surgery. But there are additional complicating factors when the one who has perpetrated the abuse is a person with religious authority. Authority attracts and focuses people's deepest longings for dependable care. Religious authority entwines this with God. The disregard of the call to dependable care which sexual abuse constitutes cuts deep into confidence in both Church and, by extension, God. So threatening is this to individuals and community alike that a very frequent reaction is to refuse to believe the victim of the abuse. The challenge of belief involves such a high degree of discomfort, anxiety and fear at every level that often it is simply easier to choose to conclude that the victim is mistaken, deluded, lying, malicious or even insane. Even to admit the possibility and to take steps to ascertain the truth, especially if the victim is an adult, is often perceived to be too difficult.

It sometimes happens that in fact the victim *is* believed, at least by some. There may already have been some unease, some concern at aspects of behaviour of the person who has perpetrated the abuse, usually unspoken. Some may even express this to the victim in private.

But the consequences of addressing the issue properly are perceived to be so disruptive to both individuals and community, and the cost so high, that nothing further may be done. Church officials, church authorities and congregations themselves may then adopt a strategy with several variants that is designed above all to protect the equilibrium of the church and defend the status quo.

The victim finds no 'good witnesses'.

The effect of such reactions to the telling of the story of abuse is profoundly damaging. Not only can it reinforce the malevolent power of memory to continue its assault after the abuse, confirm the victim's pervasive sense of being 'bad' or 'flawed' and further disintegrate the self, it actually constitutes another form of abuse – and that in a place above all where sanctuary and healing are supposedly offered. It cannot be overemphasized that in reflecting on their experience of abuse, Christian people who have survived abuse speak repeatedly of their sense of betrayal at their treatment by the Church. It is a particular irony that a group of people who, more than most, need this sanctuary and healing are very often the least likely to receive it! For many, if it does not lead to complete loss of faith, it certainly terminates their relationship with the Church.

To feel completely alone and abandoned, blamed and shamed for the wrongdoing of another, is a soul-destroying experience. Elie Wiesel, survivor of the Holocaust, has said, 'What hurts the victim most is not the cruelty of the oppressor, but the silence of the bystander', and psychiatrist Judith Herman writes:

> It is very tempting to take the side of the perpetrator. All he asks is that the bystander do nothing. He appeals to the desire to see, hear and speak no evil. The victim, on the contrary, asks us to share the burden of pain. She demands action, engagement and remembering.[8]

Too often, instead of finding sanctuary – a place of safety and justice in the Church – victims of abuse are forced into silence, guilt and a sense of personal responsibility for what has happened, and the potentially complex, far-reaching consequences. They are punished by the fear, threat or reality of breaking ranks with the conspiracy of respectability. Meanwhile, too often, the one who receives sanctuary (whether consciously or otherwise) is the offender, who is rarely held accountable or sanctioned for their behaviour (if indeed it ever comes to light), but enjoys the refuge of collusion and ignorance, and the comfort of continuing in positions of trust and responsibility.

The Church, of course, has theological and liturgical categories for responding to the assault of memory on the structure of personality, however that assault comes about. It is the moment of despair and abandonment, the time for confession, the call to conversion, to a new direction. But this is not always as clear as it seems, and the forms are not always unambiguous.

Our understanding of God as all-powerful in relation to memory may even compound suffering: thus this reflection on the collect for purity:

> **Almighty God**
> *I didn't know you*
> *you were so insignificant*
> *compared with him*
> *the one who abused me . . .*
> *He was almighty*
> *he held the power*
> *over me – he was*
> *so much bigger*
> *you see.*
> *You may have*
> *created but*
> *he destroyed*
> *my world.*
> **To whom all hearts are open**
> *How vulnerable you made me*
> *wide open in my deepest self*
> *yet you did not give me any safety strategies*
> *through your blindness to the realities*
> *of your world*
> *my heart was ripped open*
> *before it was full grown*
> *and was it divine arrogance*
> *that kept you from intervening*
> *from owning me*
> *at the point of violation?*
> **All desires known**
> *But there was no desiring*
> *only repulsion and shame*
> *I guess in your holiness*
> *these undesirables cannot be known.*
> *Is that why you were silent?*
> **And from whom no secrets are hidden**

> *but there were secrets*
> *and they were hidden*
> *embedded inside of me*
> *for years*
> *and never once*
> *did I hear you say*
> *you knew what was going on.*
> *Do you know how scary it is*
> *to feel more knowing than you?*'

The tyranny of God over memory, or God's intolerable silence in the face of it, is not just personal but political. At the heart of the Judaeo-Christian Scriptures is the memory of deliverance, salvation.

> *Remember you were slaves in Egypt . . . remember you were slaves . . . remember how you were in the past . . . remember who you were . . .*

The litany of memory runs through the Bible like a heartbeat.

But what if the problem is not that you forget you were a slave? What if the problem is that you cannot remember anything else?

A critique that ridicules established power

The assault of memory is also the problem of language. This has been a central tenet of the various liberation movements of modern theology. The historical experiences of racism, sexism, sexual violence, colonialism, poverty and degradation have been remembered in the body. But because they are the history not part of history, finding the language to recollect them has been difficult and certainly within the Christian Church controversial.

Language is a powerful tool. It describes and symbolizes and shapes our images and perceptions of God, of people, of the world. It encodes understandings of power. The language we use in worship (especially in singing) and preaching, in theology and testimony, does not describe the nature of God who cannot be contained within the confines of human language (though it may describe attributes of God) but above all describes the nature of our relationship with God.

Historically, the relationship of people with God has been described in ways that emphasize to an extreme degree our experience of the *transcendence* of God. The relationship has also been conditioned by the social and political structures of human power, and has emphasized the *power* of God in such terms. This emphasis on transcendence is heightened when it is translated into images of the *might* of God; our language for worship abounds with military metaphors.

And the relationship has been conditioned and shaped by a view of familial relationship which is hierarchical, vertical and masculine – Father, Son and Holy Ghost. All of us, male and female alike, may be acceptably described as sons of God and brothers of one another, or as children. All other relational titles are still considered to be at best unusual and at worst unacceptable, though there are in fact many biblical images of God that are motherly, feminine or nurturing. The family language for God emphasizes the *patriarchy* of God.

Some of these titles and images may hold great value for people. Their significance may not be related to their actual meaning, but more to their familiarity or their metaphorical impact in certain situations. Nevertheless, this language shapes at a deep level the nature of our relationship with God, and makes it one that does not necessarily represent the culture in which people are attempting to live out that relationship. And for some, the language and the naming may, at an involuntary level, prove an insurmountable barrier to ever hearing the language of love. All they can hear is the language of fear and shame. All they can recollect is the memory of abuse.

We need to find language and images for worship and theology that allow us to relate in a fuller way to God, so that we may also name our experience of the *immanent, empowering God* who is in *solidarity* with people who are marginalized or silenced, and a language of relationship that suggests mutuality, equality and a wider vision of being family rather than the property and posterity model that is the bottom line of patriarchy.

Language reflects the dominant patterns of a culture. But it also reinforces them. If we leave the naming of our relationship with God so one-sided, so distorted, then we are complicit with a context in which abuse, concealment and disregard for the vulnerable flourish.

Liturgy is the work of the people. 'The people' includes many who are survivors. Surely as part of the people of God they might also expect to have their experience, their hopes and regrets, their gifts and wounds, their words and images represented in the offering of worship and preaching. By what authority and in whose interest are they excluded? Or is it the case that the Church institutionally does not, in its heart of hearts, trust the silenced people, may even fear the challenge they present?

The song and dance of the women

This silencing by the Church has made it even more important for survivors to have safe places in which to share their own stories and to have 'good witnesses', places for the voicing of pain, perhaps for the first time.

We told our own stories –
That's all.

We sat and listened to
Each other
And heard the journeys
Of each soul.

We sat in silence
Entering each one's pain and
Sharing each one's joy.

We heard love's longing
And the lonely reachings-out
For love and affirmation.

We heard of dreams
Shattered
And visions fled.

Of hopes and laughter
Turned stale and dark
We felt the pain
of isolation
and the bitterness
of death.[10]

People who have survived abuse speak of the importance of doing nothing for quite a while but telling their stories and identifying their own needs. Experience suggests that here churches really struggle to respond appropriately (see also Chapter 5). It requires a willingness to be open and vulnerable, to listen, to tolerate silence and acute anxiety, to let go of the wonderful Christian need to *fix* things. It requires the capacity to lay aside the need to justify one's existence or beliefs, or to colonize the teller's feelings. It requires refusing to put forward answers to every unsolved question.

For when people attempt to break the culture of silence, whether it is the silence that conceals the abuse of power in any form or the silence of their own disempowerment, it is important not to underestimate what has been described as 'the ordeal of testimony'. It takes more time and patience than our busy churches usually allow to do what Quakers call 'hearing people into speech'. But again and again, survivors speak of the relief and hope which happen when they can speak, and be heard and believed. And for many women especially, it has been important to go beyond sharing stories into the creation of rituals, ceremonies and liturgies which use song and dance, art and drama, signs and symbols, as a way of reclaiming sacred and free space, of challenging the abuse of power and of standing in solidarity with those who have experienced abuse and are on the journey of healing.

There is still a long journey ahead in recognizing that many men also suffer from abuse, and in finding expression for this in a religious context. But liturgical resistance and good witnesses are crucial factors in working through surviving to thriving, and in addressing difficult issues of repentance and forgiveness.

The integrity of the body

Christian theology incorporates some difficult (and often contradictory) ideals when it comes to addressing the question of the integrity of the body. These include:

- the Eden myth of innocence
- the patriarchal ordering of human society
- the complementary partners
- the indissolubility of marriage
- the virgin mother
- the submissive wife
- the consecrated celibate
- the obedient child.

All of these have been interpreted at different times in ways that have turned the ideal into a nightmare. All of them have been used to legitimize sexual abuse, including every kind of non-consensual sex, incest, sexual torture, the abuse of minors and sexual humiliation and degradation. All of this is found in the Bible.

Subsequent theologians have not made the discussion any easier; Augustine of Hippo taught that original sin is transmitted by sexual intercourse. And the tyranny of dualism in Western thought and culture has been well documented. Today, however, supported by research in the human sciences of biology and genetics, some theologians argue that the idea of two sharply differentiated sexes is largely a social creation, unsupported by any natural order, and requiring constant vigilance and coercion for its maintenance. It is not difference *per se*, but the way that difference is used to systematize subordination, which has normalized the possibility of violence and abuse in gender relations. The story of Adam and Eve, as archetype and model of God's order, has embedded gender dualism in our social and ethical arrangements, by presenting it, not as a matter of cultural construction, kept in place by human convention and decision, but as inescapably *natural,* and therefore beyond the scope of human manipulation or revision.

What is the connection between this, and the reality of sexual abuse? If romantic love is based on the religious theory that it is natural for a sacrificial, loyal, enclosing female nature to *complement* a self-possessing and masterful male nature then sexual desire becomes associated with the self-destruction of subordination and the self-aggrandisement of domination. Men become real men by overwhelming, penetrating, possessing and controlling women. Women become proper women by submitting and serving. The Old Testament's 'texts of terror' (as Trible calls them) are all about women as instruments who can be used, abused, then discarded, forgotten or killed. But the legitimate marriage relationship, as described in the law and history of the Jewish people, exhibited many of the same features: men 'took' wives as part of their economic wealth. Adultery was essentially a crime against another man's property. Wives had no rights of possession over their own physical or sexual integrity. This has been a widespread cross-cultural reality: until very recently, the possibility of rape in marriage has not been recognized in Scottish or English law. Even scriptural uses of the marriage metaphor to describe the relationship between God and humankind are based on models of patriarchy not mutuality.

And the traditional Christian understanding of marriage has often seemed to regard permanence as its highest value, even when that is likely to compromise the safety, health, emotional and spiritual well-being, and sometimes the lives, of women and their children. It is possibly now the only institution which seriously suggests that it is somehow the duty of women to deliberately put themselves in danger of rape and other forms of criminal physical and sexual abuse. It is wrong to consider women expendable in this way. Moreover the Church needs to be aware of the profound damage that can be caused to children by exposure to an abusive environment even though there is little excuse for such ignorance now. And there remains the question of whether abusive men have really been helped to spiritual maturity and growth by making it possible for them to continue in their abusive behaviour.

This history has been the hinterland for the operation of three forces which make the construction of a Christian case for bodily inviolability and integrity extremely difficult without a challenge to dearly held orthodoxies; a rather unholy trinity of *purity, property and power.*

Non-consensual, non-mutual sex is a spiritual and psychological invasion as well as a physical one. Virginia Woolf's resounding twentieth-century plea on behalf of women for 'a room of her own' has a resonance with 'a womb of her own'. For most women, in most times, their reality has left little or no space for that room. Only in prayer or dreaming was it really safe to draw the lines that say: 'so far, and no farther. Beyond here is private, inviolate.' Other than that, it has been woman's duty, and supposed to be her delight, to merge, to suffer, to have the lines drawn for her, and, when necessary, to permit the lines to be blurred, or even obliterated. There are numerous biblical examples of this.

Karl Barth, convinced that the ethics of divine command required unconditional female submission, suggested that if women remain quiet and obedient in the face of male oppression or violence, this would win men to repentance for their misdeeds. Such is the pathological advice that has given comfort to so many abusive men in home, church and community, while burdening their victims with the hopeless task of responsibility for changing bad male behaviour. It is less likely now that clergy will advise women to stay in unchanged abusive relationships, though it still happens enough to give cause for concern. But many are unrealistic in their optimism about the possibilities of change in abusive behaviour. This is not generally supported by the findings of programmes to rehabilitate those who have perpetrated sexual abuse, which show low rates of change, and require a long time. The truth is that women – in marriage and other institutions – have been treated as shock absorbers, endlessly expected to give up their own living space, to accept and conceal the marks of possession on their bodies, minds and spirits.

We are becoming only too painfully aware of the extent of abuse of the most vulnerable, including children, that has gone on under cover of the patriarchal blanket. We are aware of the culpable abuse of boundaries within pastoral relationship. We are aware of the infantilization of lay people that the Church has been complicit with. We are aware of the dependency relationships that create emotionally and spiritually stunted laity and clergy alike. We are aware of the injustices that have been inflicted on those who are different, who do not conform. We are aware of the policing of pleasure that has ruined so many lives. Patriarchal structures do not encourage maturity and integrity. Father does not always know best. That we have often enjoyed the security of a benevolent paternalism does not provide sufficient response to the critique that suggests that coercive strategies are no longer appropriate. That we ourselves have not done these things does not exempt us from the responsibility of having been part of the religious culture that allowed them to happen.

Coming to light

It may be worthwhile at this point to ask exactly *what* is the nature of the Christian Church's investment in secrecy, and why this should seem to be so important. The New Testament is full of images of light, of transparency and openness; Christ is, we believe, light to the world. And he himself warned of the dangers of secrecy:

> Whatever is covered up will be uncovered, and every secret will be made known. So then, whatever you have said in the dark will be heard in broad daylight, and whatever you have whispered in private in a closed room will be shouted from the housetops. (Luke 12.2-3)

The Church is painfully learning the truth of this in regard to sexual abuse.

The reality of judgement is a note that resonates through the great prophetic voices of the Old Testament. These voices call the people of Israel to account for their crimes, including the oppression of the weak by the strong and the enslavement of children. Now we know very well that nearly three thousand years later, these have not disappeared from the face of the earth, and we rightly stand in judgement against them, condemn them, may be actively involved in campaigning against them. By the authority of Scripture, with the authorization of Church and tradition, we read the prophetic texts against a world which practises such things, and the world is found wanting.

But at this point, it may be important to remember that the prophetic words were actually addressed quite specifically to the community of faith, to the people of the covenant. Their motivation was rooted in a passionate belief that the covenant relationship of God with the people of Israel demanded that the relationships of the people with each other should reflect and replicate that covenant. To use a rather crude spatial analogy, the covenant was horizontal as well as vertical. And therefore the priests of the covenant were particularly culpable for suggesting that pious practices, religious rituals and sacrifices, visiting holy places or indeed any kind of formalism that left social morality unaffected could avert the awful reality of God's judgement. It was a dangerous illusion to suggest that no harm could befall a people chosen to receive the covenant. It was precisely because they were people who had been liberated by the Exodus, had received both the Law and the promise, that they were particularly under judgement. Of all people, they were the ones who should turn from oppressing and enslaving others.

And as followers of Jesus, sharers in the new covenant, we too have to take a relationship to the judgement of the world. By the authority of Scripture, Church and tradition, we stand in judgement on the world and find it wanting. But that judgement is a two-edged sword. For in confronting the world with our texts and dogmas, we are in turn confronted by the world, which shows us to ourselves as Church.

The Christian Church has such an appalling record of abusing power that profound humility is called for here. But the ability to walk humbly with God depends on our willingness not so much to judge as to be judged. Nobody likes being judged, either individually or collectively. We all want to believe we are justified in our beliefs and practices. We don't enjoy shame or humiliation. But sometimes, however hard we evade or avoid, the world just does it to us. To be creature, one among many, is to come face to face with our limitations. We are not God, and God is not just an idealized version of us. God is other, and speaks to us in other voices. The Church's judgement of the world, sometimes expressed as if we had a monopoly on divine truth, is in truth that which holds us most to account. Unless the Church engages with its own internal challenges, it will not have either the integrity or the credibility to speak with authority.

The silencing that many people who have been abused experience in the Church is allied to the secrecy. It is noteworthy that Jesus links visibility to audibility, being heard, in his admonition against secrecy. Silencing and invisibility are consequences of secrecy. If we are constantly informed of the need for secrecy, even threatened of the consequences if we break the secrecy, then of course, silence is the result. It is exactly the same process that the person who abuses creates and relies on. That is a sobering thought for all of us who care about the Church. For this culture of secrecy and silence depends on all of us going along with it, giving it tacit consent. As with other unhealthy diseases of the body, so with sexual abuse, we end up in a state of denial. It's there, it is immense, it inhibits our movements and freedom, it affects everybody's lives – but we don't acknowledge it, we don't talk about it, we just pretend it isn't there and work round it.

There is a crucial work of discernment needed here, so that we can distinguish between an appropriate reticence and sensitivity and an unhealthy secrecy and silence. We are, all of us, far more than even the sum of our parts, and none of us should ever be reduced to just one aspect of our existence. We want to be able to live our lives as people who are citizens, parents, artists, gardeners, as people who can bake a cake or speak Spanish or play table tennis.

And there is something graceful about sexual reticence, about keeping some things private, intimate, especially coming from an overly sexualized culture like ours where the often unappealing sexual practices of strangers assault us everywhere we turn. And there are few people who, given the choice, would not prefer to tell the secrets and break the silence in a loving, supportive environment with one or a few people, rather than in the pages of a tabloid newspaper.

And sometimes there is a natural desire to protect those wrongly accused, or to stop the mud sticking to others round about. Unfortunately, the mud has already stuck, and secrecy only makes an alienated public more suspicious.

Other reasons for the secrecy that leads to silencing, however, are less acceptable, though they may be understandable. A concern to present the best possible image of the Church may lead to the repression by secrecy of all that does not enhance that image. We want to believe in a perfect Church, not least because of our knowledge of our own imperfections. But the light will inevitably and ultimately show up the folly of this kind of secrecy. Nothing stays repressed forever, and when it is eventually laid bare, the knowledge of the covering up becomes an additional cause of disrepute.

Sometimes the secrecy is a result of fear and prejudice and the judgement of hypocrisies which will do anything rather than face the wounds in their own hearts. Sometimes it results from a theology which has taught people to be ashamed of their own sexual needs and desires, of the conflicts that arouses in them, and of being confronted in others with what they dare not acknowledge in themselves. Sometimes it happens because people are simply ignorant of what is happening to others, or about the seriousness of that, or of the difference they could make by speaking out.

And sometimes, the secrecy arises from the need to hold on to power. If the Church is seen as less than perfect, then its high authorities too may be seen in that way, and its power may be undermined.

In all of this, there are profound gospel questions to be asked about our understanding of the nature of the Church, of salvation and grace, and of the extent to which sin is understood as not just being about acts of commission but also about acts of omission. At the very least, we do not want to keep ending up in a place where the sinned against are sacrificed to preserve the image of perfection, and where power rather than love and compassion becomes the defining characteristic of the Church.

The integrity of the gospel

> *Whoever welcomes in my name one such child as this, welcomes me. But if anyone should cause one of these little ones to lose his faith in me, it would be better for that person to have a large millstone tied round his neck and be drowned in the deep sea. (Matthew 18.5-6)*

Children were important to Jesus. He honoured them, valued them, healed them and included them in his ministry as subjects with their own agency, just as he, at the age of twelve, demonstrated. And when adults were annoyed because they were making a noise in the Temple, he described them as offering perfect praise. Their protection and well-being were of paramount importance to him, and his engagement with them is characterized by kindness and gentleness. He was unequivocal in his condemnation of those who hurt children, and endangered their ability to trust.

The issue of child protection is not the main business of this report. It is a considerable step in the interest of children that most denominations now have comprehensive child protection strategies in place. However, it is worth repeating here that the sexual abuse of children, including sexualized contact with them, is always criminal, and never justifiable in theological, or any other terms. It is an offence against the gospel.

One of the characteristics displayed by sex offenders against children is the capacity to distort religious teachings, texts and values to offer spurious legitimization for abuse. While this distorted thinking is not within the power of the Church to control, it raises grave questions about how approaches to Scripture can sometimes reinforce it. The Bible contains within it many stories, which constitute a catalogue of the most appalling sexual crimes against women and children, and these have been cited by offenders to justify incest, rape and other forms of sexual molestation. An overly undiscriminating approach to Scripture has often meant a reluctance to name these for what they are, that is, stories of sexual abuse. But until we are prepared to do so, and be very clear about it, there will be those who claim that their actions are justified because 'they did it in the Bible'.

There are some frightening aspects of these stories from the perspective of those who have survived which are not just about the fate of those abused, terrible though that was. First, no one in the stories as they are recorded cares about the survivors; their suffering is not regarded with compassion or regret or even anger. There is no loyalty or care for them. They do not matter. The only offence considered is that given to the honour of the men to whom they were attached. And second, it has taken the Christian Church nigh on 2000 years to notice that no one cared about them. This is our holy book, but we have read it with blinkers. We have read it through the eyes of powerful men, and it has materially affected the ways that survivors have been treated for centuries.

Perhaps as a counterbalance to the considerable damage and suffering which has been the result of taking scriptural texts completely out of context and applying them in inappropriate and ill-informed ways, churches might test such texts against the life and teachings of Jesus to discern whether they are indeed consistent with the gospel message of good news to the poor, liberty to captives, sight to the unseeing and freedom for those oppressed. For indeed, we believe that those who are survivors of sexual abuse are survivors of oppression, and that Christ on the cross as victim identified himself with them precisely because they too are victim. To deny them is also to deny Christ.

'If one part suffers . . . '

Nothing demonstrates more clearly the truth of Paul's teaching on the integrity of the body than the narratives of sexual abuse. In the context of the body of Christ, no one is unaffected by this betrayal of trust. And the healing of the body too places demands on the whole community of faith. If we are genuinely to share the joy of the body, we must also be prepared to respond to the suffering.

For some survivors of abuse, the Church has indeed been a source of support, comfort and empowerment. But for too many, in their desolation, the hard-heartedness and rejection of the Church have been devastating. One woman said:

> Public opinion rests with the man – the assumption is that he is blameless as a man of God. Eventually one is so desperate that this is of no consequence, but it still hurts when church people ignore you or are cold to you. It feels so unjust.[11]

A time for forgiving?

One of the most difficult areas for survivors is the question of forgiveness. The granting of forgiveness and the experience of being forgiven are central to the Christian life. But precisely because of this, it is vitally important that the nature of forgiveness is not diminished, held lightly, or used to get anyone out of grappling with hard questions. Many survivors speak painfully of being exhorted to forgive their abuser, and of being blamed for their own suffering, for the abuser's suffering and for everyone else's suffering if they fail to do so. Once again, the survivor may find herself or himself needing to 'rescue' others by her or his actions. Most find themselves completely unable to do so, at least in the short-term, and once again have to carry the burden of failure.

It is worth reminding ourselves of exactly what survivors are being asked to do here. Marie Fortune notes that: 'Sexual assault is much more than just a disagreement. It is an experience of terrorism. Being forced sexually against one's will is the ultimate experience of powerlessness, short of death.'[12] And it is also worth remembering that even Jesus did not himself forgive his executioners, but asked God to do so. In the story at the beginning of the report, the point when it was suggested to Sylvia that forgiveness in this instance was for God to grant, was the moment when her true recovery became possible, when she was relieved finally of responsibility for her abusers, and freed from the 'hook' of their continuing power over her.

Nor can forgiveness be understood as a formula or panacea that in some unspecified way wipes out the past. Many survivors of sexual abuse find they cannot forgive, not because they do not want to, but because the injustice and trauma they have experienced has never been acknowledged or put right. For others, survival has been possible only because they have denied what they really feel, have taken responsibility for the behaviour of others and pretended everything was fine. But for healing and wholeness to happen, it is critical for the survivor to name the abuse clearly as not their own fault. Where forgiveness by the survivor is possible, it is as part of a long process of recovery.

It is not our intention to enter into lengthy discussion of the conditions under which forgiveness may be possible, whether repentance is a precondition or not, and who makes these judgements. We believe that attempts to coerce people who have survived abuse into forgiveness are at best misguided and at worst abusive. To urge or expect the one who has suffered sexual abuse to forgive the person who has abused is destructive unless the situation has been thoroughly resolved, the evil denounced, the perpetrator made to accept responsibility for what he or she has done and the victim restored to strength.

In some traditions, forgiveness may be sought through the confessional. We recognize that, whatever its undoubted strengths, the confessional itself has been grievously abused by those who have perpetrated abuse, who have used its guarantee of confidentiality to salve guilty consciences without any commitment to change of life, and for whom its offices have become part of the structure of abuse. This has left the confessional open to charges of complicity with abuse, and scandalized a public which has perceived the Church as once again shielding those who have perpetrated abuse, and as putting the maintenance of its own forms and dogmas before the safety and well-being of those who are abused. This is in no one's interests. Whether in the formal setting of the confessional, or in the more informal context of the chosen 'confessor figure' it is cheap grace.

We remain convinced that the same principles apply in all petitions for forgiveness, that is, the acceptance of responsibility, a genuine commitment to conversion of life demonstrated by the willingness to make restitution in whatever way is possible at cost to the petitioner, and the readiness to vindicate the victim. This is the model of Zacchaeus, and of the woman who anointed Jesus.

> The great love she has shown proves that her many sins have been forgiven. (Luke 7.47)

Forgiveness is also a crucial question for congregations affected by abuse. Penny Jamieson, Anglican Bishop of Dunedin, New Zealand, writes helpfully in terms which would also apply to others who have abused and been abused from positions of trust in the Church. While fully recognizing that the primary abuse is that suffered by the person who has been abused, for which they were not responsible, she points out the secondary abuse which results from the inappropriate urging of forgiveness – for which people do have responsibility:

> It is not uncommon for people facing up to the reality that their priest has sinned grievously to move very rapidly into forgiveness mode, and then be ready to continue as if nothing has happened. But the sin *has* happened, a very great deal of suffering has been inflicted, and it cannot be eradicated or healed by 'cheap grace'. Indeed, for the Christian community to show a willingness, even an insistence on acting out the formulas and behaviours of forgiveness before they acquire some real meaning, some real grace, is to collude in the abusive behaviour. Forgiveness becomes denial. It effectively says (what the priest is almost certainly saying) that it was a trivial matter, that the abuse was not significant, and that it is best soon forgotten. That may not be the intention in urging forgiveness, but it may well be the consequence.

An abused conscience

The silent victim of such a strategy is the priest's own conscience. For a priest who can behave, often repeatedly, in such a way has often done so by deadening his conscience, achieving a state in which there is no longer any self-accusation, no longer any sense of self-criticism or self-reproach. What could have been an opportunity for personal growth leads instead to a further decay of conscience which can make further abusive relationships with other people more likely.

An abused woman

Cheap grace and cheap forgiveness also further victimizes the woman concerned. Not only does it disregard or trivialize the abuse that she has suffered, it also further alienates her from the Christian community which has been the context of that abuse. For, usually, when a pastoral relationship is sexualized the woman loses her faith community, because she can no longer feel safe there. Cheap forgiveness greatly increases the danger she can expect to encounter there.

An abused church

Such actions also deepen the damage done to the Christian community, for the abuse of a particular woman becomes an abuse of the whole community when it ties them into patterns of deceit and secrecy. The offer of easy forgiveness to the offending priest, which buys into this syndrome, dignifies in a quite unjustifiable way the response of deception and secrecy. It also diminishes our understanding of what God can do for us, for God can forgive the enormity of our sin: we do not need to trivialize it or resort to reductionism. It can be faced in all its gravity and it can be forgiven, without denial, at the depth of truth.

It may well be that the demand for forgiveness that is cheap and quick is the natural response of people who cannot face the full horror and the tragedy of what has happened. It is a way of masking anger and the discomfort that anger brings. But it has to be faced . . .

Real love is never based on protecting people from their own truths, because if we do that we hold them in their own deaths instead of enabling real growth towards spiritual maturity.[13]

Deliverance ministries

One disturbing aspect of response to sexual abuse, which has received a considerable amount of publicity in recent times, has been the practice of so-called 'deliverance ministries'. Most of the publicity has focused on instances when this kind of ministry has had extremely negative, and in some cases catastrophic, consequences. While it is not within the scope of this report to explore deliverance ministries in detail, nevertheless, since they impinge directly on sexual abuse issues, some comment is warranted.

The theme of deliverance, as already noted, is a dominant one in the Bible. The term is used to describe the activity of God in human history towards the deliverance of people from their sufferings, and has the connotation of rescuing, saving or setting free. In particular, it refers to and resonates with the deliverance of the people of Israel out of the bondage of slavery in Egypt, as told in the Exodus story, and then with their subsequent deliverance from other forms of bondage, both material and spiritual. In the Old Testament, the word is most commonly used in the sense of rescuing or 'snatching away' of people *out of* the power of their enemies, and it is understood that in all situations, God is the only effective deliverer. Superior military capacity is, in biblical terms, no guarantee of rescue from bondage. Indeed, it is sometimes when Israel is powerful and wealthy that it is most enslaved. In the New Testament, the word most frequently used has the significance of handing over *into* the power of others, as with Jesus' own deliverance into the hands of the authorities.

But in all of these, the dominant note is that of 'the good news of deliverance', as announced in Isaiah 61, and reiterated in Luke 4, in Jesus' 'Lukan manifesto'. To be set free, to find a liberating space in which to breath fully and unrestrictedly, to have new energy released for the living of life in all its fullness, to aspire to justice and joy – this is a hope which those who have experienced abuse, and those who support them, would fully affirm. So it is particularly disturbing that some of the manifestations of deliverance ministries are profoundly abusive in themselves, and rather than bringing healing actually reinforce the original hurt. This is especially the case when exercised by people with limited or inadequate knowledge and understanding of the effects and consequences of sexual abuse, and moreover when exercised in contexts in which the operation of power dynamics is not acknowledged.

Sexual abuse is a criminal activity committed by one person against another. It is wholly extrinsic to the person who is abused. Evil is not transmitted to another by 'implantation'. The person who is abused is never responsible for their own abuse; though that expression of distorted thinking is often used by the person who abuses. 'She made me do it'; 'He wanted it really'; 'She seduced me', are all common enough justifications used by people who abuse, even when the 'she' is ten years old! One of the difficulties with deliverance ministry is that sometimes it colludes with the person who abuses, sees the problem as lying in some moral or spiritual defect of the person who has been abused (or even in 'demon possession'), and sees the solution as lying in the 'deliverance' of the abused person from their defects, sins or possession. Apart from the fact that this allows the person who abuses to avoid taking responsibility for their criminal and abusive behaviour, the damage it causes to the abused person is incalculable. It simply reinforces their feelings of worthlessness, shame, guilt and dirtiness. It can cause permanent psychological harm, destroy all potential for healthy relationships and lead to destructive behaviour and even suicide attempts.

Another difficulty can be that the essential problem is located by the ministers in the failure of the abused person to forgive the abuser. If only they could forgive, so the theory goes, all would be well, and they would feel released. The failure to forgive therefore becomes the 'sin', the problem, and it is their own hard-heartedness that they require deliverance from. In such a situation, all the issues we have already considered with regard to forgiveness apply, with the added dimension of a 'deliverance' or 'exorcism' process which is in itself intensely traumatic and often physically brutal. Again, responsibility for making everyone else feel good – abuser, family, community, and often the minister (who may have status and authority interests invested in the 'success' of the deliverance) – is placed on the abused person.

The abusive character of some deliverance ministries is accentuated by the fact that the context in which they happen is usually intensely patriarchal and authoritarian. That is to say, they simply replicate the existing power structures which have given rise to the abuse in the first place. Rather than strengthening and affirming the worth and ability of the abused person to be the subject of her or his own life, and increasing her or his agency and capacity to make free choices, they objectify and weaken the person, set her or him once more at the mercy of powerful people. And since these ministries often take place within wholly unaccountable contexts, with no supervision, parameters or constraints and little transparency, the harm they can do goes unchecked.

People who have been abused often experience themselves as being in a prison, and that prison is not one that can be broken out of simply by force of will (otherwise almost all of them would have done that). But release cannot be brought about either by simplistic formulae that suggest: (a) that the prison is one of their own making, because it is not, or (b) that spiritual superheroes can break the person out of prison using the same terrifying weapons that put her or him there in the first place – a strategy that is likely to leave the person standing traumatized and shocked by the blast, unable to move to step over the rubble. The only genuine way of helping someone to gain release from their prison is to find out what the key is that will open the door, and put it into her or his own hands. This means that it is necessary to give time and attention and gentleness, not to telling the person what they need, but asking them what they want, staying with the answers, even when they seem unacceptable to us, and accompanying someone through the long process of discovering what is healthy for them.

Though liturgies and rites of healing can be intensely meaningful and helpful for people who have been abused, therefore, they should always reinforce structures that empower the people, and the people themselves should be enabled to set the agenda and the timetable for them.

Compassion and justice

Mercy, compassion, love and justice – especially for the vulnerable and oppressed – these are surely the qualities which the Christian community is called to demonstrate. Compassion means to suffer with, to share the pain and struggle and resistance. It is rooted, specific and informed care, which is a deep expression of God's loving purpose. Compassion arises from *involvement*. It begins with listening. This is hard work. It requires an open heart, a clear mind and endurance. It is always tempting to look for excuses and rationalizations, so that we can dismiss or justify the suffering of others. But the experience of hearing, touching, feeling and responding to the pain of others is the key to change. The Hebrew word for God's compassion means 'womb love'. And from such engaged compassion flows justice.

The Revd Dr Marie Fortune, director of the interdenominational Center for Prevention of Domestic and Sexual Violence in Seattle, USA, has done more than most people to raise awareness of sexual and domestic violence in the Christian community. She maintains that there can be no healing from sexual abuse without justice, and outlines these elements as stages in the process of making justice.

First, there must be *truth-telling*: giving voice to the reality of the abuse; we have to hear this truth, acknowledge it and condemn it as wrong. But our expression of compassion should not be to take away control from the victim – to ride in on our white chargers and solve the problem. We must be willing to act as advocates – people of trust who help survivors to understand and explore the options for action – and as companions on the long journey through the desert. It is our responsibility to protect the vulnerable, and once aware of the potential for abuse, we must take steps to prevent further harm – both to the original victims, and to others who may be vulnerable. If we do not do so, we are colluding in the harm.

The next stage is *accountability* – a fair and open process for testing allegations, and the imposition of official sanctions against those who betray their sacred trust. Negative consequences provide an opportunity for the abuser to acknowledge and take responsibility for what he or she has done, and to 'get a new heart and a new spirit'. They are also essential to the healing of victims. What is damaged or destroyed by sexual abuse can never be fully restored. Nevertheless, there should be restitution – as a symbolic and practical acknowledgement of the harm done, and helping to repair the damage. This can be financial recompense, legal or counselling bills.

The ultimate goal of justice is *vindication*. This is not a matter of revenge, but a recognition that the key to physical, emotional and spiritual healing from violation is to be set *free* from the many layers of suffering which the abuse has caused.

At present, most of our Churches have neither the informed awareness, nor the commitment, nor the appropriate structures and processes, to make justice for those who suffer abuse within the Christian community. Indeed, there are many people of goodwill who are deeply concerned and distressed that this should be so. They struggle with inadequate expertise, archaic processes and the built-in biases of male-dominated institutions; they experience discouragement, resistance, confusion. People and congregations become depressed, angry, disillusioned. There is no binding up of wounds for all who are implicated – victims, perpetrators, and the wider community.

The Japanese theologian Kosuke Koyama has said:

What is love if it remains invisible and intangible? Grace cannot function in a world of invisibility. Yet in our world, the rulers try to make invisible the alien, the orphan, the hungry and thirsty, the sick and imprisoned. This is violence. Their bodies must remain visible. There is a connection between invisibility and violence. People, because of the image of God they embody, must remain seen.[14]

Many people who have been abused leave their churches and continue to do business with God elsewhere, or not at all. But this is not an uncomplicated decision. For the Church that offers hurt also offers healing. Part of what it means to be a world Church, to be part of the body, is the recognition that if one part suffers, all the other parts suffer with it. The wound of the daughter of my people wounds me too. Increasingly, people who have been abused will not readily go back to a time when they would accept silencing and humiliation at the injunction of the Church. They have recognized that to do so is not only to accept a devalued status as human for themselves, but is to be made to be complicit in injustice and in the harming of children and adults. They wish to refuse this complicity. But this does not mean their wish is to see abusers in their turn degraded, dehumanized and controlled. They want there to be instead a culture that does not glorify violence, coercion, control and manipulation, that does not represent it a thousand ways every day as an ideal of strength and power.

We are beginning, slowly and painfully, to recognize that our Churches are institutionally racist, institutionally sexist; the journey to recognize our institutionalized abuse of power is an even longer one. Part of that journey has been the struggle for people who have been abused to distinguish between the God who, in Jesus Christ, loves, affirms and believes in them, and the Church which all too often doesn't. Survivors stay because they love Jesus. They know that:

> during his life here on earth, Jesus visited the towns and villages and saw with his own eyes the problems facing the people. He saw poverty, the inequality, the religious and economic oppression, the unemployment, the depression, the physically ill and the socially unclean. His heart was filled with pity. He pronounced what his mission was all about: he came to preach the good news to the poor and to release those who are captives and give health to those who are ill.[15]

In him, they see the possibility of a new kind of community, a true community of women and men.

In searching for hints of that true community, people all over the world have been reading the Bible and the history of the Church from another angle, rediscovering the hidden histories, the silenced voices, the notes on the margins. They are seeking the God of Jesus Christ, the motherly God who comes close in the Word made flesh. They are seeking the women and men whose spirituality is one of hope and tenderness, of courage and compassion, of inclusion and protection. And with eyes fixed on Jesus, we also begin to see the outlines of another Church, a safe place for those on the margins, those who have experienced abuse, a Church in which Jesus is embodied. This is not about having a 'victim' theology. It is about the conviction that the power of resurrection and the power of the Spirit, which is the power of love, are never power *over*. Power over is what Jesus voluntarily relinquished, choosing rather power *to* and power *with*.

As Christians, we are neither just individuals nor collectives. We are persons in community. But the reality of any community, wherever and whatever it is, is that 'if one part suffers, all the other parts suffer with it; if one part rejoices, all the other parts share its joy'. We are bound up together. That basic fact of our belonging together in Christ, who is our only unity, is demonstrated time and time again in those survivors, who, precisely because they share one another's suffering, can share one another's joy with undivided hearts. The resurrection life we are raised to is not only a personal life, it is a shared one. To be in Christ is to be part of the body of Christ. He is our communion, our right relationship. And,

> the communion's need for health and mercy is inseparable from my own need for health and mercy. To remain in communion is to remain in solidarity with those who I believe are wounded as well as wounding the church, in the trust that in the Body of Christ the confronting of wounds is part of opening ourselves to their healing.'[16]

We want to finish by recalling another story. The story of an oppressed, vulnerable woman whose voice breaks the culture of silence; who exposed the conflict between the theory of justice for all, and the practice of decisions in favour of the powerful. Her plight was acute, and she called out to God to hear her cry. The odds of the system seem stacked against her, but in the midst of all her adversaries who try to put her off, make her invisible or silence her, in the domain of male control, her voice continually, persistently, cries out for justice and vindication. She blows the cover of those who have coopted the system of justice for their own ends. She calls the judge to accountability. She has received no compassion, and expects none, but she is determined to claim her right. And her refusal to give up, to stay out of sight and out of mind, to disappear quietly, is rewarded with justice (Luke 18).

CHAPTER TWELVE

Issues of liturgy and materials for worship

In the Preface to the Alternative Service Book of the Church of England published in 1980, the then Archbishop of York, the Most Revd John Habgood wrote that 'Christians are formed by the way in which they pray, and the way they choose to pray expresses what they are'. In the book of alternative services of the Church of Canada which was produced in 1989, it was stated that 'Liturgy is a principal process by which the Church and the gospel are brought together for the sake of the life of the world'. It is therefore particularly important that the Churches in seeking to minister more effectively to those who have been sexually abused and also in striving to root out from their institutions abusive practices, should constantly be aware of the powerful influences of the language of worship.

For many people the constant and uninterrupted use of language which is exclusive and used repeatedly can be intimidating or even aggressive (e.g. Almighty and Everlasting God, Lord of all Power and Might, Eternal King, All-powerful Judge, Everlasting Father, Lord and Father of Mankind). Intimidation and aggression do not give life to the people of God called to grow in wisdom and understanding. We need to use the full range of biblical images for God, the tender and nurturing as well as the powerful. All this is particularly true for women, girls and boys who have been sexually abused especially those who have been abused by powerful figures in the Churches.

The use of these symbols and metaphors of power are not only painful for those who have been abused, they can also have a deep effect on clergy who are abusers as they strengthen within them the false sense of their own power as representatives of God.

It is important that these matters are taken seriously both in the regular worship of the Churches and also most especially in any services which are seeking to minister to the needs of those who have been sexually abused.

In the book *The Courage to Tell*[1] produced by CTBI, Christian people who have survived abuse wrote about the particular importance to them of the use of inclusive language. Many survivors have great difficulty imaging God as 'Father', or even Jesus as brother. If you have been sexually abused by your father or brother, these images are just too difficult. Changing them to 'Mother' might work for some, but if you were sexually abused by your mother, or feel your mother should have known about the abuse and done something, having a Mother-God can also be problematical! Some metaphors are therefore out of reach for some survivors, so alternatives may be needed. All Christians would benefit from finding different ways of expressing our relationship with God and each other. Using one way exclusively means it is automatic, so we are not thinking about what we mean.

In the same book they commented that although there are many special Sundays or special services dedicated to various issues, such as Prisoners' Sunday, Homeless Sunday and Racial Justice Sunday, there were no special Sundays or special services for those who had been abused except for those arranged by CSSA. People who have survived abuse would be enormously encouraged if churches and communities would provide sensitive and caring worship services so that survivors could feel included and remembered. Those who would like to consider arranging such worship services might be helped by the suggestions and the worship material that we offer below.

Suggested format for services

Welcome
opening song
opening prayer
scripture reading
quiet music to meditate after reading (optional)
survivors speaking; talk, poem or song
all sing another hymn or song together
drama and/or other form of activity
prayers of intercession
second reading (optional)
homily (optional)
hymn/song
closing prayer
closing hymn/song

One suggested Introduction

Call to worship

Leader: *Come to Him for He is Light.*

All: No darkness shall overcome us.

Leader: *Come to Him for He is Truth.*

All: No falsehood shall deceive us.

Leader: *Come to Him for He is Love.*

All: No hate shall destroy us.

Leader: *Come as you are and He will make you as you will be.*

All: We shall be renewed by Him.

Leader: *Come to Him for He is the door.*

All: By Him, if we enter in, we shall be saved.

Leader: *Come unto Him*

All: And we shall find rest.

Light in the dark places

A candle is lit and given

Survivor, let the light of this candle be for you the light of God, as you meet the darkness in the deep places of your being. See the hidden things, the creatures of your dreams, the storehouse of forgotten memories, the gifts you never knew you had been given.

Touch the wellspring of your life, and hear your own true nature and your own true name.

Take the freedom to grow into that self, the seed of which was planted at your making . . .

*Listen to the language of your wounds. Do not pine away
in the pain of them, but seek to live from the depths of
them. Make the extent of your desolation the extent of
your realm . . .*

*Take into your arms your wounded frightened child within.
Give her your adult caring strength, for your child has
protected your gifts until the time they can be given and
not be betrayed . . .*

May your only wounds be these:

*the wound we cannot avoid because we belong to one
another and feel and hear the murmur of the world's pain;*

the wound of a sense of compassion for others;

*the wound of a sense of longing for God, the source of life
and love deep within us and beyond us . . .*

Jim Cotter[2]

Alternative introduction to worship

Call to worship

*We begin our time of worship in the name of God
Warmth and Light for us
Fountain whence we can draw strength
Refuge who enfolds us and heals our soul. Amen.*

Prayer

*God, we give thanks for your promise,
that our bodies and souls shall be whole.*

*Give us sufficient strength to recognize our boundaries
and firmly to say 'No' when they are violated.*

*Free us from guilt and sin
that keep us silent when violence happens.*

Be at our side, when we loudly accuse the torturers
and violators.

Through Jesus Christ, our Brother,
who has righted the violated and despised
and has given them self respect.

Amen.

Hidden Pain – a liturgical response

In the name of the Trinity – Creator, Saviour and Holy Spirit
In whose loving image we are all made
May Christ reveal the light of truth
To strip away the masks of pain.

Light a candle

By your power, Creator God, we have been formed
In love and for love
By your incarnation, Jesus Christ
The loveliness of our human bodies is affirmed.

Carried by your healing spirit
We come, in all our vulnerability
Bearing within ourselves the marks and scars
Of rejection
Criticism
Hatred
The wounding words and the cruel taunts
Seared into our souls, our very sense of self

Remind us who we really are.

Each person in the group, sitting in a circle, speaks a word of acceptance and wholeness – choose your own, in addition to or instead of these suggestions. Each has a nightlight or candle to light as she/he speaks.

Precious
Strong
Capable
Gifted
Valuable
Beautiful
Enduring
Courageous
Loving
Loved

From the shackles that bind us
Set us free

From the hurt that breaks our hearts
Set us free

From the fear that can rule our lives
Set us free

From those who want to harm us
Set us free

From the masks that hide our pain
Set us free to recognize ourselves in your image.

Amen.

A short liturgy for survivors

1989

Tonight we offered fruit for thanksgiving
Lit candles for intercessions

I offer this fruit in thanksgiving that I am learning to be angry
I light this candle for women who are survivors of abuse.

But God, I couldn't do it.

My prayers would have exposed me.

I hope you understand.

1999

Today we gather together in thanksgiving
Lighting candles as symbols of our prayers.

We acknowledge our righteous anger
and our loss.

We acknowledge the process of growth
and healing.

I light this candle for all who are
survivors of abuse.

I light this candle for the triumph of
hope over despair.

(God
It was not you I feared)

I don't want to know

I don't want to know about sacrifice
sin, and death.
Price paid on a cross.
Demands on me.
No.

Jesus suffering with me,
walking beside me.

God knowing, understanding, hearing,
accepting.

Maybe.

A thousand thousand small deaths

A thousand thousand small deaths
Blows to my spirit
Wounds to my soul
Hurts to my body
Entanglements of mind
Humanity reduced, destroyed.

A thousand thousand tiny resurrections
My spirit uplifted
My soul rested
My body healing
My mind refreshed, enlightened
Humanity restored, reaching for freedom?

A new life?

Redeemed?

I don't know.

The specifics of the Christian faith pass me by.

But I think perhaps I'm learning
Something of death and resurrection.

A hard irony

A hard irony, either glorious or terrible;
twelve hours after writing
that I cannot accept sacrifice on a cross,
I am distraught because I missed a service
where they sang
'I know that my redeemer liveth'.

Full Circle

1989

A worshipping group.
Prayers thought, felt.
Fear
Prayers unspoken
Heard by God?

1999

A worshipping group.
Prayers thought, felt.
Fear diminished.
Prayers spoken, shared.
Heard by others.
Heard by God.
I made peace
with my silence.

Iona Community[3]

Two Litanies for church members

Litany one

Let us see and hear the truth

For the truth will set us free
Reveal to us the patterns of how we collude and cover up

For the truth will set us free
Reveal to us the patterns which damage and fragment us all

For the truth will set us free
Reveal to us the patterns of individual and institutional
violence

For the truth will set us free
Reveal to us the patterns that will help us to tell the truth

For the truth will set us free
Reveal to us the patterns of your love and justice

For the truth will set us free
Reveal to us the patterns of how to live together in truth

For the truth will set us free

Jayne Scott[4]

Litany two

We are here to end the violence,
Yes we will!
We are here to break the terror,
Yes we will!
We are here to heal the wounded,
Yes we will!
We are here to help each other,
Yes we will!
We are here to make a new beginning,
Yes we will!
We are here to change the system,
Yes we will!
We are moving out together,
Yes we are!
We are creating a new world that is safe and happy
Yes we are!
Where women, men and children can live together without fear,
Yes we will!
The end of the old, the beginning of the new.
This is the time!
The end of terror, the beginning of safety.
This is the place!
The end of silence. The beginning of protest and change.
We are the ones, and we will do it
Yes we will!

(end of a healing ritual for abused women)
Rosemary Radford–Reuther[5]

Poems

Woman without a name

Woman
without a name,
raped and abused
until break of day
then taken limb by limb
through the length of the land.
What symbolism is this?
What do I hear
in your silences?

Who questions your abuse
and the crime
against female sexuality
when the only question is misuse
of man's property?

Can I stand in solidarity
with your pain
and let the silence be
wordless?

Is your silence
louder than the cry
from the cross?

Joy Mead[6]

A Poem

See me
when I stretch out
my invisible arms towards you.
Hear me when I whisper without words.
You are probably the only one
I have an ounce of faith in.
Will you talk with my voice,
give muscle and strength to my arms?
Will you help me give words to
the forbidden
that of which I cannot speak?
Can you help me
to clasp my hands in prayer
and clench my fist
to fight?
See me: I want out
through thick walls of secrets.

Written by poet EH.[7]

Prayers

I have been sinned against

I became a victim, I was blamed
and bore the guilt myself.
Before you, my God, I absolve myself
of the guilt which was not mine
and distance myself from it.

Margareta Melin[8]

Inscription

Take from my instep
The skein of damage
That has threaded its way through my life
Like a tightening cord.

Take from my body
The wounds of unloving
That puncture and bruise

Like a scarring sword.

Take from my mind
The dark engulfing
That has judged my life
Like a damning word.

Take from my soul
The unbelieving
That has made you seem
Like a lost God

Rosie Miles[9]

A short liturgy entitled
'Walking with God in sorrow and need'
Prayer

Tender God of love,
Blazing with anger at injustice
Weeping over human folly
Yearning for wholeness for all your children
We come before you now
Seeking your gift of peace
From the places we inhabit.

Some of us exist in the shadows
Oppressed and abused in body, mind or spirit
Entangled in webs of darkness and despair
Pretending all is well,
behind closed doors,
fear reigns.

We drown in confusion and our own knowledge cannot be
relied on
Hope is lost and the future cannot be imagined.
When we are tempted to lie down and give in to the
darkness
Give us strength, and send us help O God.

Possible sung response

Kyrie or spoken response

Come now God
Strengthen the faint-hearted and support the weak
Tear down our prisons

**Lead us in your paths of justice and truth
Make us instruments of your peace.**

*Some of us do not want to see what is in the shadows.
We find it hard to believe those who gather the courage to
witness to it.
It disturbs and distresses.
It questions what is at the heart of each one of us.
It threatens our ordered lives.
It exposes a dark side of our Christian community
When we would rather shut our eyes and turn our heads.
Give us courage to face the darkness, O God.*

Response: sung or spoken as above

*Some of us here cast shadows
Knowingly or unknowingly.
In many different ways, we may deny others their right to
their full humanity and flourishing.
Let us look into our hearts and see if this is true.*

Silence

*As we hear the witness of our wounded sisters and brothers,
we acknowledge where and when we have done wrong
and ask to be shown the path to peace.*

Silence

*On all who have sinned
and are truly sorry.
The God of love and justice and peace
pronounces pardon
and gives grace for new
beginnings.*

So be it. Amen

Penny Stuart[10]

A Blessing for the Way

May God,
Strong woman-worker,
Leveller of mountains and builder of highways
Carve out with us a road to peace.
May Jesus, Friend of women, and embodiment of Wisdom
Travel with us through darkness and into the light.
May the Spirit, healer and liberator
Comfort, cajole us, and lighten our hearts
Celebrate with us as justice and peace join hands.

Amen

A closing hymn: We shall go out

We shall go out with hope of resurrection
We shall go out from strength to strength go on
We shall go out and tell our stories boldly,
Tales of a love that will not let us go.
We'll sing our songs of wrongs that can be righted
We'll dream our dreams of hurts that can be healed,
We'll weave a cloth of all the world united
Within the vision of a Christ who sets us free.

We'll give a voice to those who have not spoken
We'll find the words for those whose lips are sealed
We'll make the tunes for those who sing no longer,
Vibrating love alive in every heart.
We'll share our joy with those who are still weeping,
Chant hymns of strength for hearts that break in grief.
We'll leap and dance the resurrection story
Including all within the circles of our love.

June Boyce-Tillman
Sung to the melody 'Londonderry Air' (or 'Danny Boy')[11]

CHAPTER THIRTEEN

Conclusions and recommendations

Conclusions

Time for Action was commissioned and written as an ecumenical report attempting to address the failure of the Churches, as yet, to respond adequately to the needs of those who are survivors of sexual abuse.

The report considers wider issues relating to sexual abuse and the Churches, looking at developments and legislation within Britain and Ireland; procedures developed to improve child protection practice in the Churches; reasons why it is hard to tell stories of abuse; ways to respond to those who have experienced abuse; implications of abuse for the families, friends and communities of those involved; factors relating to abuse as it occurs in church contexts and ways of responding to those who abuse. A major chapter is given over to an extended theological reflection on many of the issues raised elsewhere in the report.

The overall conclusions of the Group responsible for preparing the report are that the Churches have begun to take seriously various aspects of the complex issues relating to the experience of sexual abuse. There is some very good practice to build on. But there is also much more still to be done. No church has yet got it all right. Some have hardly started the journey.

It is clearly important that churches have good policies and procedures for child protection and for dealing with allegations. It is equally important that churches consider carefully how they respond to the needs of those who have abused. Great care needs to be taken when trying to involve people with a history of sexual offending in the life of a church community. However, the Group were left with a clear impression that the major gap still to be filled is in the area of responding to those who have experienced abuse. Their stories are very hard to tell, but have helped the churches become more aware of the need to take child protection and good practice in pastoral care seriously. Nonetheless the adults who have experienced abuse still do not generally find the Church a safe place or a listening community. Little is provided for those who have experienced abuse, either directly or indirectly. Much more could be done to offer pastoral and spiritual support.

The implications of taking these issues seriously are far-reaching. They affect every church community and every church member. There are particular responsibilities for those in roles of leadership or influence. There are specific developments needed in areas such as the recruitment, selection, training and ongoing support and supervision of those who exercise pastoral ministry within the Church.

Some of the implications are about doing things differently. Others are about doing new things. Some will have financial implications. But the writers of this report are convinced that while the talking and thinking need to go on, and will do so for years to come, now is particularly a *Time for Action.*

List of recommendations, chapter by chapter

1   Introduction: how Time for Action *came to be written*

1. That this report be widely read and discussed within CTBI and member Churches and that its implications be considered and acted upon by churches individually and ecumenically at local, regional and national level.
2. That material be produced by each member Church to enable all church members to become better aware of these issues and alert to their responsibilities as individuals and community members.
3. That, wherever possible, any work done by churches in response to this report include survivors of abuse, whose contribution on these as on other matters is crucial.

2   In the beginning was the story...

4. That the member Churches of CTBI be willing to listen to survivors of sexual abuse as they claim their right to justice.

3   Preparing the way: agreeing definitions and parameters

5. That the work being done by other groups within the member Churches of CTBI on the development of child protection policies and procedures be endorsed; and that all churches be encouraged to take the implementation of these most seriously.
6. That the Church Life Secretary of CTBI should identify ways to monitor developments in this area in order to enable the member Churches to keep their policies and procedures under review.

4   Setting the scene

7. That in their consideration of issues of sexual abuse the member Churches of CTBI take into account the way in which the social climate regarding matters of sex and sexuality has changed in the last 50 years.

5   It's hard to hear but harder to tell

8. That the member Churches of CTBI consider how to become and provide safe places, so that opportunities may be made for those who survive abuse to tell their stories.

9. That the member Churches of CTBI develop better listening within their communities and become aware of local agencies and individuals able to offer more specialized help to people who have been abused if they request it.

10. That the member Churches of CTBI respond to the requirements of the disability discrimination legislation and go much further to make sure that disabled people who have been abused are enabled to communicate their stories and concerns within church communities.

6   Listening well to what's hard to tell: responding to those who have experienced sexual abuse

11. That the member Churches of CTBI make available appropriate and acceptable pastoral care for those who have experienced sexual abuse.

12. That those involved in the provision of retreats consider working with survivors of abuse to provide appropriate retreats for those who have experienced abuse.

13. That member Churches of CTBI consider providing adequate funding for CSSA and other such self-help organizations.

14. That the member Churches of CTBI develop policies and procedures relating to allegations of sexual abuse and that these policies and procedures be widely publicized. A clear notice should be displayed in every church building regarding these policies and procedures, the availability of redress and an independent contact person or number.

15. That Churches nationally and regionally identify and make available to ministers and others lists of support groups, agencies and other resources appropriate to the needs of those who have experienced abuse.

7   Ripples in a pond

16. That Churches produce clear guidelines and support structures to help those dealing with the effects of abuse on a family and within a community, including a church community.

8   Abuse within the Church

17. That the member Churches of CTBI look again at their complaints and discipline procedures to ensure they are just and that there are appropriate and accessible mechanisms for complaints of sexual abuse to be made, heard and dealt with.

18. That member Churches in their ministerial training programmes provide adequate education concerning appropriate professionalism, the dangers of misuse of power and the importance of maintaining boundaries in pastoral relationships.

9   Causation: sexual abuse in the Church

19. That those responsible for the recruitment, selection and training of ministers within the member Churches of CTBI consider the implications of this report for their areas of responsibility.

20. That within the member Churches of CTBI, training programmes for ministers incorporate mandatory study and discussion on these issues, along with appropriate training on child protection matters and pastoral training in how to deal with incidents of sexual abuse and how to respond to the needs of survivors.

21. That within the member Churches of CTBI, training in human sexuality, relationships and human development be provided in theological colleges and seminaries, on courses and in continuing ministerial education.

22. That within the member Churches of CTBI, provision be made for the equivalence of 'supervision' for those working in pastoral care; and accepting such supervision be a requirement for the continuation of ministry.

23. That within the member Churches of CTBI, increased 'pastoral care' be provided for those involved in ministerial function.

24. That within the member Churches of CTBI, therapeutic resources be provided in an accessible manner for those with individual psychological/sexual problems in line with 'employee assistance' programmes.

25. That additional investigations be conducted into a functional theology of sexuality and human relationships that can incorporate the distinctive features of modern society, including patterns of courtship, marriage and the diversity of domestic units.

26. That within the member Churches of CTBI, strong action be taken to end the culture of silence and secrecy that surrounds many aspects of ministry and church life and to encourage transparency in procedures.
27. That clear codes of professional ethics and structures for accountability be developed by member Churches and applied to and by those placed in positions of pastoral care and leadership.
28. That member Churches encourage the development and promotion of 12 Step Sexual Recovery Programmes and other behavioural regimes to facilitate change and foster healthy relationships.

10 Responding to those who abuse

29. That CTBI and member Churches make known to the UK Government their concern at the closure of the Wolvercote Institute and emphasize that it and/or similar facilities are essential and their insights need widely publicizing.
30. That CTBI and member Churches make clear to the Government and statutory agencies their willingness to be involved in multi-agency approaches to the rehabilitation of sex offenders in the community.
31. That member Churches make use of the work that has already been done to consider and develop procedures for reincorporating those who commit sexual offences into church communities. Such procedures need to include proper supervision, risk assessment, 'contracts', etc.
32. That member Churches commit themselves to working closely with other appropriate agencies when seeking to incorporate sexual offenders within Christian communities.
33. That member Churches in England and Wales take note of the results of the pilot schemes of 'Circles for Support' once they are available and consider whether and how to become more involved in this model of support.

11 'Christ is like a single body': some theological reflection

34. That member Churches of CTBI commit themselves seriously to consider the theological section of this report and develop ways of engaging local groups and individuals in such theological reflection.
35. That member Churches give urgent consideration to the development and enforcement of appropriate codes of practice regarding healing and 'deliverance' ministries.

12 *Issues of liturgy and material for worship*

36. That the member Churches of CTBI give careful consideration to the effects of the use of language on those who have been sexually abused as well as others in congregations and make appropriate changes.
37. That local churches make opportunities to pray for those who have been sexually abused and consider whether it would be helpful in their locality to offer special services for them.

Appendix 1

Material for Churches considering how to respond to those who have perpetrated abuse

The Diocese of Southwell, in the Church of England, produced their own guidance on child protection issues in a booklet entitled *Children and Young People First.*

They followed this up with another publication entitled *Recognizing, Responding, Managing and Pastoring Risk* (1999) which contained new material about relating to those who had perpetrated sexual abuse. Recently this material has been brought together in a new Code of Practice for the Diocese. Section 5 is concerned with 'Perpetrators of Child Abuse'. It contains the following pastoring guidance, which is reproduced with permission.

5.7 Pastoring Guidance

The main focus of pastoral care will be for the individual. It is important to be aware of and accept the view of most professionals who work with perpetrators who believe that they will need maintenance counselling for the rest of their lives. Thus in theological terms recovery from the "sin" of sexual abuse is a daily ongoing process.

A small number of committed people can play a valuable role in this by:

- Following the advice given by those with knowledge of or who are working with the perpetrator.
- Seeking guidance and supervision from these professionals, the Diocesan Child Protection Co-ordinator and the church leader/incumbent.
- Continually reaffirming to the perpetrator that it is because of their care for him that they will not tolerate abusive behaviour any more, that they are committed to supporting him as he makes efforts to change his offending pattern of behaviour.
- Giving the message that, because they love their children, and because they love the person, they will not allow him to be in situations where he might be tempted to abuse.
- Helping the perpetrator to understand and accept that repentance is much more than saying sorry – it is an ongoing turning away from the destruction caused to another child of God, attempting to make amends, and offering restitution.

- Encouraging him to co-operate with the legal system if he has been convicted and in participating in any treatment programme available to him.

Pastoral care to others:

On occasions, the incumbent or church leader will need to ensure that pastoral care is extended to others – especially should a perpetrator or alleged perpetrator become publicly known within the church. This might involve:

a) **Those who are party to the contact and/or work with the individual**

- checking that people remain comfortable with the information and are coping with the issues raised
- ensuring that those committed to supporting the individual get the opportunity for reflection
- sustaining people's contribution.

b) **The wider congregation**

- considering how to inform people of the details and how to help people handle the information
- recognizing that this may for some people release memories, and for others remind them of other undisclosed incidents (possibly involving other people).

5.8 Example of a parish contract with known perpetrator of abuse

At the end of a page giving a case study and helpful guidance there is the following summary:

The priest makes it clear to a fictional person, Steve, that:

a) there needs to be an agreed 'contract' between Steve and the priest which outlines proscribed activities within the church.
b) though the contract may need to be modified from time to time, it will always stipulate that Steve cannot work with children or be part of the church's work amongst young people.
c) the contract will be known to the priest, the church wardens and the youth minister only.

Appendix 2

Outline of training course on the pastoral care of those who have experienced abuse and those who have abused, suggested by the Group

Definitions and parameters
The nature of sexual abuse
The experience of the survivor
The experience of the perpetrator
Awareness in ministers and community
Appropriate responses to survivors in church community
Appropriate responses to perpetrators in church community
Education and training for ministers and community
Structural/Institutional responses
Managing allegations of abuse
Assessing risk
Deconstructing the 'groomed' environment
Recognizing:

For the survivor the processes of	Denial
	Despair
	Anger
	Shame
	Depression
	Survival strategies
	Justice
	Healing
For the perpetrator the processes of	Denial
	Atonement
	Treatment
	Reparation
	Justice
	Reconstruction of trust
For the church, the processes of	Denial/culpable ignorance
	Shock
	Disgust
	Fear
	Lack of competence
	Unconscious collusion
	Preventing abuse
	Forgiveness.

Notes and references

1   Introduction: How Time for Action *came to be written*

1. Home Office, *Safe from Harm*, HMSO, 1993.
2. M. Kennedy, *The Courage to Tell*, CTBI, 1999. Christian survivors of sexual abuse tell their stories of pain and hope.
3. S. Parsons, *Ungodly Fear: Fundamentalist Christianity and the Abuse of Power*, Lion, 2000.

4   Setting the scene

1. Home Office, *Supporting Families*, HMSO, 1998.
2. Methodist Church, *Domestic Violence and the Methodist Church: The Way Forward*, Methodist Church, 2002.
3. Home Office, *Safe from Harm*.
4. UK Government, *Working Together to Safeguard Children: A Guide to Inter-agency Working to Safeguard and Promote the Welfare of Children*, HMSO, 1999.
5. Home Office, *Safe from Harm*.
6. Church of Ireland, *Safeguarding Trust*, Church of Ireland Office, 1997, 2nd edn 2000.
7. Salvation Army, *Safe and Sound*, Salvation Army, 1996, 2nd edn 2000.
8. Lord Nolan, *A Programme for Action: Final Report of the Independent Review in Child Sexual Protection in the Catholic Church in England and Wales*, Catholic Bishops' Conference of England and Wales, 2001.
9. National Children's Bureau, *Taking Care: A Response to Children, Adults and Abuse for Churches and Other Faith Communities*, National Children's Bureau, 1992, 2nd edn, 1997.
10. Lord Nolan, *A Programme for Action*.
11. Lord Nolan, *A Programme for Action*.
12. Catholic Bishops' Conference of England and Wales, *Healing the Wounds*, Catholic Bishops' Conference of England and Wales, 1994.
13. Methodist Church, *Report on Sexual Harassment and Abuse*, Methodist Church, 1997.
14. CSSA, *Safe Church: Safe Children*, BM-CSSA, 1997.
15. Kennedy, *The Courage to Tell*.

5 It's hard to hear but harder to tell

1. P. M. Sullivan, M. Vernon and Scanlon, *Sexual Abuse of Deaf Youth*, American Annals of the Deaf 3, 1987.
2. UK Parliament, *Question asked by David Hinchliffe* MP, Hansard, Christmas 2000.

8 Abuse within the Church

1. Child Protection Task Force – Conference of Religious in Ireland (CORI), *Ministry with Integrity: A Consultation Document about Standards in Pastoral Ministry*, Tabor House, Milltown Park, Dublin 6, Ireland, 2001.
2. CSSA, *Clergy or Minister Sexual Exploitation of Adults in the Pastoral Relationship: What You Need to Know*, MACSAS, c/o BM-CSSA.
3. R. M. Gula, *Ethics in the Pastoral Ministry*, Paulist Press, 1996.
4. Gula, *Ethics in the Pastoral Ministry*, p. 104.
5. Child Protection Task Force – CORI, *Ministry with Integrity*, p. 13.
6. Child Protection Task Force – CORI, *Ministry with Integrity*, p. 16.
7. M. R. Peterson, *At Personal Risk: Boundary Violations in Professional–Client Relationships*, W.W. Norton, 1992.
8. Child Protection Task Force – CORI, *Ministry with Integrity*, p. 16.
9. P. Rutter, *Sex in the Forbidden Zone: When Men in Power Abuse Women's Trust*, Aquarian, HarperCollins, 1990.
10. Gula, *Ethics in the Pastoral Ministry*

9 Causation – sexual abuse in the Church

1. *Daily Telegraph*, Thursday 6 November 1997.
2. Wolf and Eldridge, 'A multi-factor model of deviant sexuality', Paper presented at the International Conference on Victimology, Lisbon, 1984; D. Finkelhor, *Child Sexual Abuse*, The Free Press, 1984; W. Marshall and H. Barbarbee, 'An integrated theory of the etiology of sexual offending', in W. Marshall, D. Laws and H. Barbaree (eds), *Handbook of Sexual Assault: Issues, Theories and Treatment of the Offender*, Plenum, 1990, pp. 257–75; G. Hall and R. Hirschman, 'Sexual aggression against children: A conceptual perspective of etiology', *Criminal Justice and Behaviour*, 19, 1992, pp. 8–23.
3. T. Ward, R. Seigart and S. Hudson, 'Good lives and the rehabilitation of sex offenders', in T. Ward, D. Laws and S. Hudson, (eds) *Sexual Deviance: Issues and Controversies*, Sage, 2002, in press.

4. J. Sullivan, 'The spiral of sexual abuse: A conceptual framework for understanding and illustrating the evolution of sexually abusive behaviour', *Notanews*, 41, 2002, pp. 17–21.
5. Editors, 'How common is pastoral indiscretion?', *Leadership*, 9.6, 1988, pp. 12–13.
6. M. Fortune, *Is Nothing Sacred?*, HarperCollins, 1989.
7. R. Sipe, *Sex, Priests and Power*, Brunner/Mazel, 1995.
8. S. Grenze and S. Bell, *Betrayal of Trust*, Praeger, 1995, p. 240.
9. P. Francis and T. Baldo, 'Narcissistic measures of Lutheran clergy who self reported committing sexual misconduct', 2002, in press.
10. T. Birchard, 'Clergy sexual misconduct: Frequency and causation', in *Sexual and Relationship Therapy*, 15.2, 2000, pp. 127–39.
11. M. Fortune, 'Is nothing sacred? The betrayal of the ministerial or teaching relationship', *Journal of Feminist Studies*, 10, 1994, pp. 17–26 (26).
12. Birchard, 'Clergy sexual misconduct'.
13. D. Stern, *The Interpersonal World of the Infant*, Karnack Books, 1998.
14. H. Lewis, 'Shame and the narcissistic personality', in D. Nathason (ed.), *The Many Faces of Shame*, Brunner/Mazel, 1987, pp. 93–132.
15. D. Nathanson, 'A timetable for shame', in Nathanson (ed.), *The Many Faces of Shame*, Brunner/Mazel, 1987.
16. P. Carnes, *Don't Call It Love*, Bantam Books, 1991.
17. R. Earle and G. Crow, *Lonely All the Time*, Pocket Books, 1989; M. Fossum and M. Mason, *Facing Shame: Families in Recovery*, W.W. Norton, 1986; T. Birchard, Unpublished research, 2002.
18. Fortune, 'Is nothing sacred?', p. 19.
19. H. Adams, L. Wright and B. Lohr, 'Is homophobia associated with homosexual arousal?', *Journal of Abnormal Psychology*, 105.3, 1996, pp. 440–5.
20. Birchard, Unpublished research.
21. Birchard, Unpublished research.
22. A. Goodman, *Sexual Addiction: An Integrated Approach*, International Universities Press, 1998.
23. Carnes, *Don't Call It Love*.
24. Carnes, *Don't Call It Love*.
25. Goodman, *Sexual Addiction*.
26. Stern, *The Interpersonal World of the Infant*.
27. O. Kernberg, 'Factors in the treatment of psychoanalytic treatment of narcissistic personalities', in A. Morrison (ed.), *Essential Papers on Narcissism*, New York University Press, 1986, pp. 213–44.
28. Birchard, 'Clergy sexual misconduct'.

29. Benyei, *Understanding Clergy Misconduct in Religious Systems,* Haworth Pastoral Press; R. Brock, and H. Lukens, 'Affair prevention in the ministry', *Journal of Psychology and Christianity* 8.4, 1989, pp. 56–62; D. Hands, 'Clergy sexual abuse', *St Barnabas Community Chronicle,* Available from Saint Barnabas Centre, 34700 Valley Road, Oconomowac, WI 53066, USA; J. Muse, 'Faith, hope and the urge to merge in pastoral ministry', in the *Journal of Pastoral Care,* 46.3, 1992, pp. 299–308; P. Steinke, 'Clergy affairs', *Journal of Psychology and Christianity,* 8.4, 1989, pp. 56–62.

30. P. Francis and T. Baldo 'Narcissistic measures of Lutheran clergy who self reported committing sexual misconduct', 2002, in press.

31. L. Booth, *When God Becomes a Drug,* Jeremy B. Tarcher, 1991.

32. W. James, *Varieties of Religious Experience,* repr. American Penguin Library, 1982 [1902].

33. The Diocese of Oxford, *The Greatness of the Trust . . .,* Diocese of Oxford, Easter 1996. The report of the Working Party on sexual abuse by pastors, p. 5.

34. T. Birchard, 'Clergy sexual misconduct', Unpublished MSc Thesis, South Bank University, London, 1998, p. 65.

35. J. Gonsiorek, 'Assessment for rehabilitation of exploitative health-care professionals and clergy', in J. Gonsiorek (ed.), *Breach of Trust: Sexual Exploitation by Health Care and Professionals and Clergy,* Sage, 1995, p. 154.

36. Birchard, 'Clergy sexual misconduct'.

37. K. Lebacqz and R. Barton, *Sex in the Parish,* Westminster/John Knox Press, 1991, p. 45.

38. A. Irvine, *Between Two Worlds,* Mowbray, 1997.

39. Birchard, Unpublished research.

40. *Guardian,* 27 October 1997.

41. Birchard, 'Clergy sexual misconduct'.

42. Birchard, Unpublished research.

43. P. Jamieson, *Living on the Edge: Sacrament and Solidarity in Leadership,* Mowbray, 1997.

44. Sipe, *Sex, Priests and Power.*

45. Fortune, *Is Nothing Sacred?;* Irvine, *Between Two Worlds.*

46. Methodist Church, *Sexual Harassment and Abuse.*

47. Centre for the Prevention of Sexual and Domestic Violence, *Information on Sexual Offenders,* 1992.

48. Bud Palmer, in *Leadership,* Winter 1988, p. 16.

49. Birchard, 'Clergy sexual misconduct'.

50. Birchard, 'Clergy sexual misconduct'.

51. Lebacqz and Barton, *Sex in the Parish,* p. 128.
52. T. Ward and S. Hudson, 'Good lives and the rehabilitation of sex offenders', in T. Ward, D. Laws and S. Hudson (eds), *Sexual Deviance: Issues and Controversies,* Sage, 2002, in press.
53. Sullivan, 'The spiral of sexual abuse'.
54. Finkelhor, *Child Sexual Abuse.*
55. Sullivan, 'The spiral of sexual abuse'.
56. Finkelhor, *Child Sexual Abuse,* p. 54.
57. Finkelhor, *Child Sexual Abuse,* p. 68.
58. P. Carnes, *Out of the Shadows,* CompCare, 1983.
59. Carnes, *Don't Call It Love,* p. 105.
60. Carnes, *Don't Call It Love,* p. 67.
61. M. Fossum and M. Mason, *Facing Shame: Families in Recovery,* W.W. Norton, 1986.
62. Birchard, Unpublished research.
63. M. Boulding (trans.), *The Confessions,* Hodder and Stoughton, 1997, p. 192.
64. Fortune, 'Is nothing sacred?'

10 Responding to those who abuse

1. Methodist Church, *The Church and Sex Offenders.*
2. Board of Social Responsibility of the Church of England, *Meeting the Challenge: How Churches Should Respond to Sex Offenders,* Church House, 1999.
3. Methodist Church, *The Church and Sex Offenders.*
4. Lord Nolan, *A Programme for Action.*
5. Board of Social Responsibility of the Church of England, *Meeting the Challenge.*

11 Christ is like a single body – some theological reflection

1. W. Brueggemann, *Texts That Linger, Words That Explode,* Fortress Press, 2000.
2. Wild Goose Worship Group, from 'The liturgy for Holy Communion. A', Wild Goose Publications, 1999, p. 80.
3. R. Williams, *Resurrection,* Darton, Longman and Todd, 1982.
4. Popular hymn, source unknown.
5. D. Harding, *Baptist Praise and Worship,* Oxford University Press, 1991, p. 755 (copyright Stainer & Bell).
6. R. Williams, *On Christian Theology,* Darton, Longman and Todd, 2000.
7. K. Galloway, 'Shame', in *Talking to the Bones,* SPCK, 1996, p. 18.
8. J. Herman, *Trauma and Recovery: From Domestic Abuse to Political Terror,* Pandora Press, 1998, pp. 7–8.

9. E. Fairbrother, 'Meditation on the Collect for Purity', in H. Ward and J. Wild (eds), *Human Rites,* Mowbray, 1995.
10. E. Gateley and R. Chinnici, 'The sharing', from *Psalms of a Lay Woman,* Source Books CA, 1981.
11. Source confidential.
12. M. Fortune, 'Forgiveness: The last step', in Anne L. Horton and Judith A. Willamson (eds), *Abuse and Religion: When Praying Isn't Enough,* Lexington Books, D and C Heath and Co., 1998.
13. Jamieson, *Living at the Edge,* pp. 117–19.
14. K. Koyama, In an address given at the WCC 8th Assembly, Harare, 1998.
15. M. Kanyoro, From an address given at the WCC 8th Assembly, Harare, 1998 and printed in *Your Story is My Story, Your Story is Our Story,* Justice, Peace and Creation Team, WCC, 1999. The book of the Women's Decade Festival, p. 29.
16. R. Williams, From an address given at the Lambeth Conference, 1998. Anglican Communion News Service.

12 Issues of liturgy and material for worship

1. M. Kennedy, *The Courage to Tell.*
2. J. Cotter, 'Light in the dark places', from *Waymarks: Cairns for a Journey. Unfolded from thoughts of George Appleton, Charles Williams and Julian of Norwich,* Cairns Publications 2000.
3. J. Hulin, 'Survivors', from *Praying for the Dawn,* a resource book for the ministry of healing, Wild Goose Publications, 2000.
4. Previously unpublished poem by Jayne Scott.
5. By Rosemary Radford-Reuther, from *Women Church: Theology and Practice of Feminist Liturgical Communities,* HarperCollins, 1985.
6. J. Mead, *Dreaming of Eden,* Kathy Galloway (ed.), Wild Goose Publications.
7. E. H. Poem, from resource leaflet of 'Kirklelig Resurssenter for Misshandlede Kvinnor'.
8. M. Melin, Prayer from *Karleken en bro* (Love-a-Bridge), 1992.
9. R. Miles, from *Praying for the Dawn,* Wild Goose Publications, 2000.
10. Previously unpublished worship material by Penny Stuart.
11. June Boyce-Tillman, *We Shall Go Out with Hope of Resurrection,* Stainer & Bell, 1993.

Further reading and study material

Child protection guidance produced by the Churches

Baptist Union of Great Britain, *Safe to Grow: Guidelines on Child Protection for the Local Church and its Youth Leaders,* 1994.

The Church in Wales, *The Cure of Souls, The Calling, Life and Practice of the Clergy.* The report of a Working Party set up in 1995 by the Archbishop of Wales.

The Society of Friends, *Safeguarding Children from Harm,* 1996. Guidelines to Quaker Meetings.

United Reformed Church, *Good Practice: Safeguarding Children and Young People in the Church,* 2nd ed., 2001.

The Church in Wales, *The Care and Protection of Children,* Church in Wales, 1997. Statement of policy and guidance for implementation.

House of Bishops, *Policy on Child Protection,* Church House, 1999.

Methodist Church, *Safeguarding: A Policy for Good Practice in the Care of Children and Young People,* Methodist Publishing House, February 2000. A Methodist response to the Codes of Practice of the Home Office and Scottish Office concerning the protection of children and young people.

Church of Ireland, *Safeguarding Trust,* 1997, revised 2000

The Catholic Church in Scotland, *Keeping Children Safe,* 1999, revised 2002. Guidelines for good practice for paid staff and volunteers who work with children, young people and vulnerable adults in a church context.

Lord Nolan, *A Programme for Action: Final Report of the Independent Review in Child Sexual Protection in the Catholic Church in England and Wales,* 2000.

CCPAS, *Guidance to Churches: Protecting Children and Appointing Children's Workers,* CCPAS 1998.

Government publications

HMSO, *Setting the Boundaries: A Summary Report and Recommendations,* July 2000 [includes Protection of Children Act 1999 and Sex Offenders Act 1997].

HMSO, *Working Together to Safeguard Children,* 1999.

Other useful books

E. Bass and L. Davis, *The Courage to Heal,* Cedar, 1991.

H. Cashman, *Christianity and Child Sexual Abuse,* SPCK, 1993.

D. P. Farrell and M. Taylor, *Silenced by God: An Examination of Unique Characteristics within Sexual Abuse by Clergy, 1997.* Requests for reprints to Derek Farrell, Cognitive Behavioural Psychotherapist, Directorate of Psychological Therapies, St Catherine's Hospital, Tranmere, Birkenhead, Wirral, Merseyside, UK.

M. Lew, *Victims No Longer: A Guide for Men Recovering from Sexual Child Abuse,* Cedar, 1990.

M. Pallauer (ed.), *Sexual Assault and Abuse: A Handbook for Clergy and Religious Professionals,* HarperCollins, 1997.

A. Peake and M. Fletcher, *Strong Mothers: A Resource for Mothers and Carers of Children who have been Sexually Assaulted,* Russell House, 1997.

T. Morrison, *Emotionally Competent Child Protection Organizations: Fallacy, Fiction or Necessity,* John Bates, Richard Pugh and Neil Thompson (eds), chap.14, *Protecting Children: Challenges and Change,* Arena.

R. C. Summit, 'The Child Sexual Abuse Accommodation Syndrome' in *Child Abuse and Neglect,* Vol 7, no 2.

Useful organizations to contact

Bristol Crisis Service for Women
PO Box 654
Bristol BS99 1XH
Tel: 0117 925 1119
This number is a National Helpline for Women –
Friday and Saturday evenings 9pm to 12.30am, Sundays 6pm to 9pm.

Broadcasting Support Services (*The Survivors' Directory 2002*)
Distribution Unit 24
Piccadilly Trading Estate
Manchester
M1 2NP
Tel: 0161 277 7000
Fax : 0161 277 7018
Support services for survivors of abuse in the United Kingdom
and the Republic of Ireland.

ChildLine
Freepost 1111
London
N1 0BR
Tel: 0800 1111
Children can also write.

CSSA (Christian Survivors of Sexual Abuse)
BM-CSSA
London
WC1N 3XX
An organization for Christian adults sexually abused in childhood.

Churches' Child Protection Advisory Services
Helpline: 01322 660011

Kidscape
152 Buckingham Palace Road
London
SW1W 9TR
Tel: 020 7730 3300
Helps parents keep children safe.

MACSAS (Ministers and Clergy Sexual Abuse Survivors)
Address c/o CSSA above.
A group for women and men sexually abused by clergy or ministers as children or as adults.

NAPAC (The National Association for People Abused in Childhood)
c/o BSS
Union House
Shepherd's Bush Green
London
W12 8UA

One in Four
219 Bromley Road
London SE6 2PG
email: support@oneinfour.org
Run for and by people who have experienced sexual abuse.

Vashti – Scottish Christian Women Against Abuse
Tel: 01738 850 995

Index

Note: Page references in italics indicate figures.

Sullivan, P.M. *et al.* 31
supervision: of clergy 24, 55–6, 77, 79,
    81, 89, 91–3, 151, 153
  of offenders 20, 56, 106, 154
  of therapists 43
  in work with children 21
support networks 1, 24–5,152
Supporting Families (Home Office) 19
survival mechanisms 39, 41, 43, 49–50,
    69
survivors: denial of abuse 47
and differing needs for therapy 38–9
seen as sinful 53, 56–7
survivors of abuse: and alienation from the
    Church 14–15, 113, 125, 128, 133
  Church services for 25, 136–49, 155
  effects of abuse on 13, 29, 36, 40,
    46–8, 49–50
  and giving of evidence 19
  identifying 27–35
  male 29–30, 60–63, 118
  and pastoral care 1–2, 10, 11, 24–5,
    38–66, 150, 152
  pathologizing of 24–5
  response to 26–37, 38, 39, 49–50,
    52–66, 70–72, 107, 112–13, 117,
    132–3, 150
  and support organizations 24–5
  and vulnerability 27, 29, 31–2, 74
  see also stories, personal
Survivors of Child Abuse (S.O.C.A.) 3–4,
    25
Survivors' Directory 24

theology 108–134, 154–5, 3, 23
  of healing 34, 35
  and integrity of the body 118–21, 125
  and integrity of the gospel 124–5
  and justice 132–4
  and overcoming of secrecy 121–3
  of sexuality 91, 123, 153
  see also forgiveness
therapy: and anger management 43
  delayed 70
  and memory 109
  need for 38–9
  and sexual difficulties 43
  see also counselling
Thomas, Gillian 4
touch: fear of 42, 66
  inappropriate 40, 64, 78

training: of church groups 61–2
  of clergy 2, 14, 23, 24, 89, 91, 151, 153
  for counselling 79
  for pastoral care 2, 35, 152, 158–9
transference 78, 80, 81
  and love for counsellor 80
Trible, Phyllis 119
trust: and children 6, 41, 124
  and clergy 73, 76, 77–9, 82, 90, 98,
    132
  in counsellors 79
  loss of 41, 46, 52, 64, 65, 68
  recovering 45, 55
truth-telling 132

Ungodly Fear (Parsons) 4
United Church of Canada 83
USA, abuse by Protestant clergy 83

Vashti 25, 168
vindication, and justice 132, 134
violence, domestic 19
virginity, loss of, and guilt 53, 54
vulnerability to abuse 12, 27, 29, 65, 74
  of children 13
  of the disabled 27, 31–3, 34–5
  in pastoral relationship 76, 80, 90

Walsh, Bishop Eamon 3
Ward, Tony, and Hudson, S. 93
Ward, Tony, and Siegart, Richard 83
Waterhouse, Sir Ronald 3
The Way Forward (Methodist Church) 19
Wiesel, Elie 113
Williams, Clifford 83, 91
Williams, Rowan 3, 109, 110–111, 133
Wolf Sexual Assault Cycle 4, 93, *94*
Wolvercote Clinic 4, 5, 84, 154
women: abused 11
  as blamed for abuse 85
  and resistance to power 108, 117–18
  sexual abuse by 11, 37
  and subordination 118–20
Woolf, Virginia 120
work with children, and fear of litigation
    20–21
Working Together to Safeguard Children
    20
worship *see* liturgy